UP AROUND THE BEND

the oral history of

CREEDENCE CLEARWATER REVIVAL

UP AROUND THE BEND

the oral history of

CREEDENCE CLEARWATER REVIVAL

By Craig Werner

Edited by Dave Marsh

SPIKE

An Avon Book

In memory of Jim Allen

For Brian Berry, Kent Lawyer, and Mike DeLong

AVON BOOKS, INC.
1350 Avenue of the Americas
New York, New York 10019

Copyright © 1998 by Craig Werner
Cover photograph copyright Jim Marshall, courtesy of Fantasy, Inc.
Book design by March Tenth, Inc.
Published by arrangement with March Tenth, Inc.
Visit our website at **www.spikebooks.com**
Library of Congress Catalog Card Number: 98-90872
ISBN: 0-380-80153-1

First Spike Printing: March 1999

SPIKE TRADEMARK REG. U.S. PAT. OFF. AND IN OTHER COUNTRIES, MARCA REGISTRADA, HECHO EN U.S.A.

Printed in the U.S.A.

QPM 10 9 8 7 6 5 4 3 2 1

CONTENTS

Acknowledgments vii

Author's Note ix

Introduction 1

1 SOUTH OF EL CERRITO 13

2 GOLLIWOGS 31

3 SAN FRANCISCO AND THE SWAMP 58

4 FROM WOODSTOCK TO COSMO'S FACTORY 99

5 JOHN FOGERTY, SONGWRITER 140

6 DEPARTURES 155

7 SILENCES   174

8 THE PILGRIM AND THE BLUES   209

Discography   232

Sources   238

Index   241

ACKNOWLEDGMENTS

Thanks to everyone who helped make this book a reality, beginning with Dave Marsh, who invited me to contribute to this series. Thanks also to Sandy and Harry Choron of March Tenth, Inc., who exhibited remarkable and much appreciated patience while I tried to dig out from under two simultaneous deadlines, and to Rachel Burd, for copyediting. Thanks to my agent, Dan Greenberg, for helping me get through the paperwork in one piece.

This book would not have been possible without the efforts of Irwin Soonachan of *Goldmine Magazine*, who established my first contact with John Fogerty, and Bob Merlis, of Warner Brothers, who made the interviews that provide the core of this book happen. I am equally appreciative of Stu Cook and Doug Clifford's decision to talk with me about subjects that continue to cause everyone involved a good deal of pain.

Numerous members of the River-Rising Internet mailing list provided invaluable assistance in locating and gathering the materials used in filling in the "old part" of the story. Howard Fields gave invaluable bibliographical assistance. I owe special debts of gratitude to Robert Aerts, Jukka Leino, Alex from Blue Meanie Records in El Cajon, California, Javier Diaz, Fred Hinnegan, John Robeson, and Graham Niven, who provided the illustrations that bring this book to life. In the midst of writing this book, I suffered a disastrous computer crash that wiped out my e-mail files, so if I've forgotten anyone from RR, it's the cyber-demon's fault. Sorry, guys.

Heartfelt thanks to Merl Saunders, Rachel Donahue, Ben Fong-Torres, Joel Selvin, and Kjell Ekholm, who shared memories, got me in touch with sources, and gave me permission to quote from their interviews with various members of CCR. Hank Bordowitz, whose CCR book is more complement than competitor to this one, was extraordinarily generous in sharing materials. Read both of us.

Closer to home, thanks to Tim Tyson, Missy Dehn Kubitschek, and Eric Schumacher-Rasmussen, whose conversation and editorial insights have been crucial to the development of my thoughts on CCR. As always, it's difficult (not to mention pointless) to disentangle those specific conversations from the ongoing conversations on music and America that involve literally dozens of students and friends, including Jim Vincent, Adam Chern, Michael and Keisha Bowman, Dave Junker, Barbara Ewell and Jerry Speir, Geoff King, Lori Leibovich, Lisa Photos, Shanna Greene, Ed Pavlic, and Robert Philipson, who played a crucial role in helping free the transcripts of the "Old Man Down the Road" trial from the California catacombs. Major thanks to Jeannie Comstock (who's convinced it would have been really cool to hang out at Cosmo's Factory) for seeing to it that the words made it out of my computer and onto the page. Investigating the CCR story has made me particularly appreciative of the support I've received from family members, including my father, Ray, and my late mother, Donna; my brothers Blake and Brian; my nephews Kiel and Jesse; my nieces—Shelby, Chelsea, Taryn, Shannon, and Jayme; my parents-in-law, George and Jean Nelson; and my sister-in-law Jonlee Peterson. And finally, as always, my wife, Leslee Nelson, and our daughters, Riah and Kaylee Werner, made room for me to work and sprinkled their own energies across everything I wrote.

AUTHOR'S NOTE

The story of John Fogerty and Creedence Clearwater Revival can't be reduced to a single narrative. It's the story of conflicting impulses, contradictory myths. And it takes place against the backdrop of an America that was redefining its own mythic identity. In telling that story, I've chosen to present a montage of statements made by the main players at the time and those made in retrospect. For the most part, the "facts" don't change much. But the perspectives change immensely. I've concentrated on issues related directly to the music, providing just enough information concerning the personal backgrounds to illuminate what seems to me the central story. Anyone wanting more details on the legal hassles and personal conflicts among the group members should check out Hank Bordowitz's *The Most Important Part Was Revival: The Unauthorized History of CCR*. In putting together this montage of voices, I have sometimes compressed materials from interviews held at the same time. John Fogerty tends to reiterate similar points in roughly the same words, so I've chosen to eliminate repetition. The date of the source interviews is included following each quotation.

INTRODUCTION: WROTE A SONG FOR EVERYONE

From the beginning, there was something deeply mythic about Creedence Clearwater Revival. It began with the name, which seemed to flow up out of the deep South, the home of Elvis, gospel, rockabilly, and the blues. In early 1969, many listeners hearing "Proud Mary" for the first time thought it was an old spiritual or a Leadbelly song they'd half forgotten, something from deep in the American grain, reinvigorated to reflect a generation's yearning for a sense of community deeper than anything available in suburbs such as El Cerrito, California, where Stu Cook, Doug Clifford, and the Fogerty brothers, John and Tom, grew up. The myth rang out in Creedence's sound, a deceptively simple rock and roll that convinced everyone who'd ever banged out "Louie Louie" at a high school dance that, given perseverance and a strong enough belief in a shared vision, they too could make it out of Lodi and onto center stage at the Fillmore. It was the yearning that made Woodstock something more than a media event, that helped millions find a shared voice for repudiating the government's lies about race and poverty and Vietnam. Even though John Fogerty sometimes felt like "an outsider in my home town," Creedence hung out in San Francisco during the Summer of

Love, played most of the major rock festivals, supported the American Indian Movement's occupation of Alcatraz, and provided the antiwar movement with a resounding voice on Top Forty radio. "Bad Moon Rising," "Fortunate Son," "Up Around the Bend," "Run Through the Jungle," "Down on the Corner," "Who'll Stop the Rain"—it's impossible to remember the sixties without the songs that earned John Fogerty his place in the first rank of American songwriters.

In 1970, at the height of CCR's success, Stu Cook expressed the sense of communal connection at the core of the group's mythic appeal: "Creedence Clearwater Revival is definitely a fifth person. Outside of the four of us." Tom Fogerty concurred: "We've been together for ten years. We've got a unity of minds. Our goal has been constant, to make it in music, but only after making it together as people." As the sixties passed into the seventies, you could hear echoes of the same dream from Sly Stone's part of San Francisco to Berry Gordy's Detroit, from the New Jersey shore where Bruce Springsteen was shaping his own version of the myth to the Stax studios in Memphis, which John Fogerty identified as his spiritual home. When CCR's "Green River" conjured up visions of a return to a place where the bullfrogs sang and the cool waters shimmered, you could almost believe all those communal selves could come true.

It didn't last. By the time "Have You Ever Seen the Rain?" and "Someday Never Comes" sounded the group's bittersweet epitaph, it was hard to remember that the ideals had ever been anything more than wishful thinking. From John Kennedy's Camelot to Martin Luther King, Jr.'s "Beloved Community" to Abbie Hoffman's "Woodstock Nation," communities fell apart; visionary ideals descended into paranoid nightmares.

Creedence was no exception. If the group's rise had been excruciatingly slow, its decline was precipitous. And the specific nature of the decline highlights both the contradictions of the earlier ideal and the reasons why the music remains as vital today as it was when Ronald Reagan was still regarded as a right-wing California crackpot. The central contradiction of CCR as communal idyll rests in the person of John Fogerty. Despite the communal myth—and there's no reason to doubt that CCR believed it was true—the real source of the group's power lay in Fogerty's intensely individual vision.

Fogerty comes as close to the spirit of the men and women of classic blues as any musician ever to come out of white America. It's not that he plays the blues as such; he reserves the title of bluesman for the black musicians whose legacy he has pursued in a series of what he calls "pilgrimages" to the Mississippi Delta. As Fogerty knows, a white kid from El Cerrito is venturing onto risky ground if he presents himself as the voice of Stovall's Plantation. But there's another way of thinking about the blues that helps explain why, for example, "Who'll Stop the Rain" and "Fortunate Son" can be considered the best blues songs written about Vietnam. Black novelist Ralph Ellison defines the blues as "an impulse to keep the painful details and episodes of a brutal experience alive in one's aching consciousness, to finger the jagged grain, and to transcend it, not by the consolation of philosophy but by squeezing from it a near-tragic, near-comic lyricism." Later, Ellison refers to the blues as "an autobiographical chronicle of personal catastrophe expressed lyrically." Speaking to the political catastrophe that California bestowed on the nation as a whole, Stu Cook recalled, "We used to joke that the blues came up the Sacramento River on Ronald Reagan's back."

Fogerty's music testifies to the accuracy of Ellison's perception that the blues speak to our dilemmas, not just as a specific music, but as a way of confronting the human condition. Beyond nostalgia, what keeps CCR's music alive is that the wellsprings of Fogerty's creativity lie not in the feeling of connection—he never released a love song until 1997—but in

Stu Cook was born in Oakland, California, on April 25. (Within hours of Doug.) Stu is a truly exceptional individual, endowed with a sharp mind, mellow disposition and distinctive sense of humor. He plays bass guitar with Creedence. At home, he is likely to play anything; on the piano it may be a Beethoven sonata or a Jerry Lee Lewis rocker. In a quieter mood he may pick the blues on an acoustic guitar, or master a new melody on the recorder.

Stu is a gifted photographer and does his own developing, enlarging and whatever else photographers do. Someday he hopes to get into motion picture making and has already been involved in several amateur films, helping with the direction and camera work.

His other interests include indoor sports, literature and selected out-of-door things. In league with John, he also enjoys riding his motorcycle, which he affectionately refers to as his "hog." Stu is probably the most adventuresome of the group, likes to travel, digs Mexico, and adds a touch of psychedelia to Creedence.

His personality fits right in with the other members. He loves to joke and play with Doug, talk politics and philosophy with Tom, or discuss business and the future with John. Educated, responsible, and a genuinely warm human being, Stu Cook is one of four unique individuals who give their all to being Creedence Clearwater Revival.

Fan club bio: Stu Cook *(Courtesy Graham Niven)*

his experiences of isolation and loss, of anger and doubt. Rock critic Dave Marsh had it right when, referring to "Who'll Stop the Rain," he wrote: "The idea that rock and roll is lighthearted good time music stops here, at the gateway to its heart of darkness." And that applies at least as well to the eighties and nineties as it did to the sixties and seventies. A hundred years from now—and I'll take any bets as to whether or not the music lasts that long—Creedence Clearwater Revival is likely to be heard as the voice of the late twentieth century, not just a moment therein.

The most basic irony in the story of John Fogerty and Creedence Clearwater Revival may well be that the rest of the band had a deeper sense of community than the man whose music made them its symbol. From the beginning, Stu Cook, Doug Clifford, and Tom Fogerty all seem to have enjoyed CCR's success a good deal more than their creative leader. Stu and Doug relished the San Francisco scene; after Tom left the group in 1971, he immersed himself in the Grateful Dead's truly communal circle, collaborating with Jerry Garcia and Merl Saunders. Cook and Clifford continued to make solid rock and roll with the Don Harrison Band, Southern Pacific, and the Sir Douglas Quintet. But none of the music they've made since CCR officially broke up in 1972 is likely to change anyone's life. Doug and Stu are at their best playing the old songs with Creedence Clearwater Revisited. No one's better qualified to play them with flair and "authenticity." In a very real sense, Cook, Clifford, and Tom Fogerty, before his death in 1990, have lived out the myth of the garage-band-made-good.

And that isn't a knock. It's true that any competent rock-and-roll band can learn to play CCR (or Chuck Berry for that matter). But the fact is that Cook, Clifford, and Tom were the ones who actually made the records. Even in the midst of the creative estrangements, legal entanglements, and personal bitterness chronicled in the later chapters of this book, everyone involved rejects the rumors that John Fogerty actually

From the time he could reach the keyboard of a piano, **John Fogerty** has lived in a world of music. He is a total musician. As a song writer, he is among the best. A brilliant guitarist, his style is his own, unmistakably. He is a no-nonsense producer able to put his albums together for about $2,000., while other rock albums can easily cost upwards of $50,000 to produce. A dynamic singer and performer, he leaves his audiences breathless. John is friendly and has a warm smile. He is quiet, but not moody. He likes a laugh but isn't a joker. He can be terribly serious, but never unpleasant.

John was born in Berkeley, California, on May 28. Contrary to popular belief, he has never been to the South except recently to perform. Any southern or delta influence in his music can be attributed to his original favorites: early Elvis, Carl Perkins, Little Richard and a host of rhythm and blues artists, including Howlin' Wolf, Muddy Waters, Lightnin' Hopkins, and many others. John owns and plays over a dozen different guitars, both acoustic and electric. He also plays harmonica, piano, organ, saxophone, dobro, slide guitar, and has a few wierd noise-makers that must have their origin in the depths of some Louisiana swamp.

Today, John does as he pleases. He is always very much into music, sometimes spending an entire week-end without sleep to write, arrange, probe and create. He enjoys athletic participation and riding his motorcycle. His dress is almost constant: levi's, western-style shirt, cowboy boots, and an army-issue field jacket. His mind seems to knife through plastics and unnecessary formalities. He is a very free individual having little care for society's restricting designs. John is more interested in tomorrow.

Fan club bio: John Fogerty *(Courtesy Graham Niven)*

Tom Fogerty has always had a deep involvement with music. It was probably Tom's influence on John that led to the formation of The Blue Velvets. Originally a vocalist knowing a few chords on the piano, Tom now displays an exacting talent on rhythm guitar. He also combines with Stu to provide back-up vocals on a number of Creedence songs. He is a dedicated musician and will practice hours on end, never stopping until he is satisfied he has perfected something he didn't know when he started.

Tom was born in Berkeley, California, on November 9. Music in all forms is Tom's life. If he's not playing himself, he's usually listening to someone else. He is an ardent reader and finds many hours of quiet enjoyment in literature. Tom and the group generally agree on two other groups as their favorites: The Beatles and Booker T and The MG's. Had fortune been different, Tom feels that Otis Redding would be the greatest singer on the scene today.

Blessed with an active mind and a pleasant nature, Tom has a long shock of blond hair, hazel eyes, and never forgets how to smile. Like the others he also enjoys active participation in sports and spends many an afternoon on the Factory basketball court.

About his relationship with Creedence, Tom says, "John and I have always been brothers, obviously. But we regard ourselves just as close friends. That's the way it is with the group, too. We seem to have a unity of minds. Our goal has been constant — to make it together in music, but only after making it together as people."

Fan club bio: Tom Fogerty *(Courtesy Graham Niven)*

played all the instruments. It's not at all clear that Fogerty, demon-haunted from the beginning, could have realized his vision working with anyone else. Although the myth of the Creedence community may not have reflected the literal truth, Fogerty clearly needed the support of friends willing to help him realize his deeply complicated musical vision. "We were there straight and sober every day for rehearsal. He could count on us. We did everything we could to make him happy," Clifford said before concluding sadly: "We never could." "It may have been John's swampy, bluesy vision," Cook added, "but we were the people who materialized the dream. We gave it the flesh and the bone."

From the beginning, however, Fogerty's interviews were much more likely to emphasize the "I" than the "we." That's the nature of a blues voice; it's about isolation, dealing with your own devils, finding a way to go on in a world where every idea of community you might have believed in has been reduced to ashes. It makes sense that while his brother was helping Merl Saunders produce gospel artist Walter Hawkins, John would be tramping across the Mississippi Delta in search of the ghosts of Robert Johnson and Charlie Patton. Fogerty's sense of life, his vision of America, had always been deeper and more complicated than the sixties myth he came to symbolize. Yet, the myth wasn't entirely wrong. Fogerty's musical vision *is* about community.

In a country torn apart by conflicts more often ignored than confronted, the vision lives in the sound of CCR's music, which testifies to the possibility of a better America than any of us—John Fogerty most definitely included—have ever actually known, a place where blacks and whites, men and women, insiders and outsiders, maybe even old friends and adversaries, can come together in a kind of spiritual communion. Looking back at his own musical heritage—he talks about everyone from Benny Goodman and Ricky Nelson guitarist James Burton to Ray Charles, and Booker T. and the MGs—Fogerty understands the communal call of the American musical tradition clearly. From the time he started giving interviews, he was nearly obsessed with figuring out his own place—and by extension the possible place of American white folks generally—in a tradition shaped largely by the songs of the slaves and their descendants. He'd always known the deeper, harder truths about the violence behind the American myth. But he had a sense that black and white might come together, if only enough people met the challenge of learning who they were, of finding their own voices. As he said when reflecting on the trips to Mississippi that helped him end a ten-year silence: "I think about what Muddy Waters really did, and he's every bit as seminal, as groundbreaking as Elvis Presley. Initially, they went to different parts of our culture, but they ended up in the same place." It's a mythic place, of course, a place where Fogerty and Bruce Springsteen, who inducted *CCR* into the Rock and Roll Hall of Fame, join their voices with those of Muddy and Elvis, Mahalia Jackson and Robert Johnson. At its best, it's the place Fogerty had in mind when he sang "Green River," the place he returned to in "Swamp River Days" on his 1997 album *Blue Moon Swamp*.

But it's also a place where everyone understands what Fogerty was getting at in "Wrote a Song for Everyone," which captures the tormenting relationship between the blues "I" and the elusive American "we" with aching precision. The imagery and the sound of the guitar take you back to the Hebrews in bondage, the Delta sharecroppers, the Oakland ghettos where "Pharaoh spins his message round and round the truth." Fogerty walks the county welfare lines and laments his isolation: "Wrote a song for everyone, but I couldn't even talk to you." But he knows that the only thing you can do is try to get the truth said as clearly as you can and hope someone hears. Fogerty isn't buying any easy reassurance. To the suggestion that "it's different now," he responds with a line that captures the heart of the blues: "Look, it's just the same." What makes

Doug Clifford, Creedence's colorful drummer, was born in Palo Alto, California on April 24. His pleasant disposition and high spirited ideals make him an absolute joy to know and accompany in any situation. He is a very warm individual with an honest love of nature and beauty. He is very serious about his profession and spends a generous portion of his free time improving his skills.

From grade school, Doug has developed a very sincere interest in science and conservation. His knowledge of botany and insects is seemingly unbounded, while his interest in conservation is almost angry, often expressing outrage at what Man has done to pollute his environment. For Doug, a fulfilling afternoon is one involving his notebook, magnifying glass, and a walk in the country. Bicycling, hiking and athletics of all kinds supplement his other activities.

On his lighter side, Doug is a fun loving sort, and is constantly joking and teasing with others. His interest in science has earned him the nickname "Cosmo" as his close friends refer to him. His 5'9", 150 pound frame boasts an abundance of exercise and top physical condition. A first class entertainer, his performances always add to the excitement of a CCR concert. About his profession Doug says, "Music for me is a highly personal form of communication, one that overcomes language barriers. If music helps people to communicate, that's important. If it makes them feel good too, as I think ours does, that's just as important."

Fan club bio: Doug Clifford *(Courtesy Graham Niven)*

Fogerty one of the great American songwriters is his ability to balance the fatalism of "Wrote a Song for Everyone" with the ferocity of "Fortunate Son" and the celebratory energy of "Green River." In truth, the myth needs them all.

SOUTH OF EL CERRITO

A lmost everyone who hears Creedence Clearwater Revival for the first time assumes they're from the South. In fact, all four members of the group grew up in the East Bay San Francisco suburb of El Cerrito. As John Fogerty commented in 1997, "there's not much Southern about that." Yet from the "swampy" feel of the music to the New Orleans twist in Fogerty's pronunciation of "bootleg" as "boo-lay," CCR's songs feel Southern. "I've thought about that for years," Fogerty said. "Where did that come from?" The answer to his meditations arrived, appropriately enough, at the 1986 Rock and Roll Hall of Fame dinner, where he delivered the induction speech for Buddy Holly. Holly was part of the initial group of inductees, alongside Elvis Presley, Ray Charles, Little Richard, Jerry Lee Lewis, James Brown, and Chuck Berry. "That was when I finally got my answer," Fogerty recalled. "I'd been thinking about this for twenty-five years. That night I stood there and either the people who were being honored were there at the same time or their posters. There were pictures of everybody all around. I looked and looked at each one of them and realized they were all from the South. Rock and roll is Southern and that's why I'm Southern. Because what I learned from was Southern. I rest my case."

The Southern voices Fogerty encountered on records and radio stations such as

KWBR, Oakland's premier R&B station, provided him with a deeper sense of connection than anything he found in the world around him, especially after his parents divorced when he was seven years old. In a 1969 Newsweek *article that introduced Creedence Clearwater Revival to the general public, Fogerty painted a bleak portrait of his home life. "I was always ashamed. I never brought my friends home," he recalled. "My room was in the basement—cement floor, cement walls. I just grabbed music and withdrew." Contrast that statement with his brother Tom's version of the Fogerty family: "We got a pretty fair deal. . . . Hell, everybody I knew came from a broken home." Where Tom, who was eleven when his father left, observed that "we came from a strict middle-class middle-income background," John told* Newsweek *that "I see things through lower-class eyes. If you sit around and think about all that money, you can never write a song about where you come from."*

So it's not really a surprise that John found his sense of community in the music of the poverty-stricken South. He described his Hall of Fame epiphany specifically as a discovery of family: "If you imitate your father and other people say, gee, you imitated your father, for you, you don't even have a choice. You just do what you see." In fact, Fogerty owed his exposure to music largely to his mother, Lucille. His first direct connection with a musical community came when his mother took him along to folk music lessons and barbecues where he met folk revival icons Pete Seeger, Sam Hinton, Mance Lipscomb, and Lightnin' Hopkins. While Fogerty remembered the "aura" of the folk scene with affection, he gravitated to an interracial family that included most of the musicians whose images sparked his awareness that night at the Hall of Fame. When he was eight years old, Fogerty imagined himself as part of that world.

John Fogerty

I remember as early as 1953, when I was about eight years old, that I was going to name my group Johnny Corvette and the Corvettes. I know it was 1953 'cause the Corvette was brand-new. I had already made a choice: I was thinking about making a career out of music. It was pretty vague. I didn't know if we were singing doo-wop or what, but the imagery of the Corvette—I was pretty psyched on that. And, of course, I was Johnny Corvette. Somehow I was the leader already. But it was a dream; it wasn't a real thing. I think I pictured myself twenty-three years old and black with a blue sparkle suit on and the other Corvettes behind me. (1993)

I was always in music. When I was two, I learned the words to "Shoofly pie, apple pandowdy, makes your eyes bug out and your tummy say howdy." I'd be dancing around church and all that—and I preferred to be alone. I just wanted it that way. When I was about three years old, I wanted to go to the moon. Me and this other kid were gonna build our own rocket ship—the world's so big when you're three, anything seems possible.

The music that we heard even before we started listening to R & B was our parents' old records like "It's a Long Way to Tiperarry." That was a record they bought. It had a pleasing melody. We played "Tubby the Tuba." We liked that. That was the music that was around the house. "San Antonio Rose." The first records that were ever given to me were Tex Ritter—"Red River Valley." My mom gave them to me when I was about four years old. "Red River Valley," that was my song.

I was given a drum when I was four, and beat the heck out of it and busted it in three days. There was a piano and a violin in the house, and I picked things out, but you can't make that kind of music on piano or violin, so in the eighth grade I got an old guitar from Sears. I remember hearing Jody Reynolds's "Endless Sleep." I had learned to play a few chords and I was *screaming* the song, and my mom came in [saying], "What are you doing?" But it was the first time that I got a rush out of playing and singing. That guitar was the first moment of realizing, "Hey, I'm gonna do this." Then I started messing around with an old high hat we had around the house. I remember practicing on all of them, trying to make all this music, like a one-man band. One day, I was playing the piano and the high hat all by myself. It was an old song by Ernie Freeman called "Lost Dreams" that had a real loud kick drum. It really got me. So I'm playing the piano with one hand and the high hat with the other, and singing the melody. And my mom comes in again and says, "What in the heck are you doing?" It was crazy, but it all made sense to me. It was this urge to do it all at once, to hear it all at once. (1969, 1985)

Piano was my first instrument, really. And I learned "Bumble Boogie," Jack Fina, and it's a 78 [released by Freddy Martin]. And I slowed it all the way down to 33. And it took me months and months. But I sat there, and I learned it note for note. No kidding. I could play it as good as that record was. I couldn't do it now. No way! But I look back at that, and I think that was impossible. That was, it was one of the most intricate records ever, really. And I've got these two hands going . . . and I learned how to play one rhythm in this hand and another in the other.

I convinced my mom that I could pay the time payments, got a catalog from Sears and Roebuck, and there was a Silvertone guitar and amp, each for thirty-nine ninety-five and you paid interest over a ten-month period so it was eighty-eight dollars total payment. About the time I got the electric guitar Duane Eddy was on the radio and he was a big influence on me. That first album of Duane's is so classic: How to make an instrumental record. Out of eleven or twelve cuts there, I think I was hearing nine of them on the radio. We used to do "Three Thirty Blues" over and over. We just called it "Blues in G." Each one of those songs had a beginning, middle, and end, like English lit or something. It was just so intelligent, and it sounded so great. I learned from Chuck Berry, Diddley, and Carl Perkins records. I also got a Burl Ives songbook to figure out the chords.

At about the same time, there was the folk music boom, "Tom Dooley," "Hill and Gully Rider," Harry Belafonte, the Kingston Trio, and on and on, mostly acoustical guitars. I actually went with my mom to some folk music guitar lessons. She took me to all the festivals and the barbecues and that was great exposure and a big influence on me. Mostly I learned the aura of folk music. I didn't learn anything on the guitar. Because mostly it was just meeting all these people. Sam Hinton, Pete Seeger, and all that. And when you're twelve, it's tremendous! And right then was when Pete Seeger was really a commie and the whole thing. I went to the Berkeley Folk Festival, and to the barbecue they had, and stood near and talked half an hour to Pete Seeger and Sam Hinton. Asked Lightnin' Hopkins for his autograph and got this scrawl from him. Mance Lipscomb was there, too. What a great potpourri of music. Folk music was like a side thing, but it was available. I could see musicians performing and having fun. I'll never forget seeing Ramblin' Jack Elliot. You gotta remember I was twelve or thirteen years old, so my voice would crack. It was terribly embarrassing. But on guitar I'd do these things the rest of the class, who were adults, couldn't. I'd show off a little. (1985, 1997)

When I was young, I was smitten by Elvis and Duane Eddy. Elvis was out, and that was like "God, what is this—voodoo or something?" Elvis was the role model back then. But there came a point when I could tell the difference between their roles; Elvis on the Dorsey show was just strumming his guitar. I've had renewed respect for him in later years. He sure strummed it great. He could really mash the guitar, and those old Sun Records have a great acoustic sound. But still, there came a time when I knew there were other guys who could play with a lot more technique and finesse. Particularly Chet Atkins and James Burton. Chet was the first guitarist I appreciated because he was the artist, the solo artist. He was the name on his records. He was obviously real good, and I liked some of his early records. Chet was more country and more elegant, and I knew that he was awfully damn good. But then James Burton came along, and he was rock and roll. He just really played the crap out of that guitar. It sounded so good, particularly on the records he made with Rick Nelson. I'm about fourteen years old and I'm thinking, "When I grow up, I want to be a really good guitar player like that." And then you go on, and you're in a garage band that plays mostly instrumentals, so we emulated The Ventures and Duane Eddy. (1997)

Doug Clifford

El Cerrito had kind of a class difference, highlanders and flatlanders, highlanders being the folks that lived up on the hill who had money and the working-class folks who lived down in the flatlands. Stu's dad was a wealthy lawyer, so he was a highlander. I was kind of a midlander. My dad was a machinist, my mom worked at Emporium Capwells, so we lived sort of on the hill but not up where the professional people lived. John was a flatlander living in a divorced home with his mother, who was a schoolteacher. That was the El Cerrito I remember.

I had a good time as a kid there, I enjoyed it. I was just learning to play drums. I loved music, I was a record collector. I knew somewhere somehow I was destined for show business. Everyone thought I'd be a comedian. I was kind of the class clown. I ended up being the band clown. I helped keep things together longer than they would have been otherwise with my sense of humor. (1998)

Stu Cook

El Cerrito was a sleepy all-white little bedroom community, a suburb of Oakland. El Cerrito was where people went to raise their kids when they didn't want to live in the city. It was middle class with barely a bit of upper middle class. But mostly it was solid middle class to lower middle class, working people. A clean town. El Cerrito has some history. It used to be a gambling town and a bootlegging town during Prohibition. My grand-parents told me you could tell cars driving up and down San Pablo Avenue with the rear end dragging on the ground, you knew the trunk was full of booze.

It comes pretty close to touching on Berkeley, which has always had a great vibe. Berkeley's had its ups and downs since hard drugs came in. It had a great folk music tradition. I got turned on to music there. My dad and mom got me tickets to Ray Charles. I was in, like, sixth grade, play-ing classical trumpet, going through one of my phases before baseball and girls. Man, when I saw that concert, I knew that was the greatest thing. Ray Charles is just the greatest thing live, him and Otis Redding.

We had great radio in the Bay Area. We had pop music that was occa-sionally playing Perry Como, but in the daytime we had KWBR from Oakland, which is an R & B station, and at nighttime we could get KRAK from Sacramento, which was country and western. The Bay Area's an amazing place musically because during World War II, when they had the shipyards here, a lot of people came from all over America who weren't in the army or navy, they came here to build ships, so there was this massive migration from the South, Oklahoma, and the Midwest. We could hear Jimmy McCracklin and Howlin' Wolf and Muddy Waters. We heard them before we heard Chuck Berry. (1968, 1998)

Doug Clifford

Living in the Bay Area, the melting pot of America, people came out to build ships in the Richmond shipyards. All these people came out, and with them they brought their music, so there was this interesting blend of rural and urban blues and Top Forty rock and roll, KYAA, KFRC. We lis-tened to the radio a lot and we were able to pick up a lot of different music right there where we lived. (1998)

"Your basic American garage band," circa 1967 *(Courtesy Graham Niven)*

John Fogerty

I went to El Cerrito schools, high schools. I went to St. Mary's for one year. I didn't fit in. I missed a lot of school from then on, really. I was practicing and stuff. At one point, in the eighth grade, I stayed home—to watch the World Series was my excuse—and I started practicing, and I ended up staying home about a month. I'm really not sure how I passed the eighth grade. Some of the teachers must have been on my side. In the ninth grade in St. Mary's, I think I missed fifty percent of the school year! And in the first half of the tenth grade, I missed something incredible. I think I missed sixty days out of the first semester, so they said, well, enough's enough. And they sent me to El Cerrito. Which is the greatest thing that ever happened. Because, well, the other two guys in the group were there for one thing. You know, the next year after that, I got straight As. I mean, it wasn't that I was dumb, I just had other interests. I didn't care about school, really. I had a year or so when I thought I was stupid. I never read Mark Twain, even though people are always comparing us to him. I did read that Tom Sawyer whitewashing the fence scene, but that's all. Dickens? Sure. *A Tale of Two Cities* and *Oliver Twist*, I loved them. I guess what I liked most about Dickens is how he identified with his origins.

Religion? What's that one guy always said when someone asked him, "Do you read music?" He says, "Not enough to hurt my playing." I'm kind of that way about religion. I was raised Catholic but not strictly so. I don't have a minister dad in my background or even a military father. It's pretty casual, it seems like a pretty normal kid's upbringing. I wasn't ruler-whipped with a Bible in front of my nose or anything. I can't say that I've really read a lot of the Bible. It's more what you hear in our culture, you know, in movies and plays.

I had plenty to entertain myself, so I didn't seek out a lot of people. It wasn't that high school tragedy trip at all. (1997)

I could see myself surviving, yeah. To me, there was never any question. The only time there was a question was when I started thinking about it too much. I started saying, "Well, everyone who tries thinks they're good. So maybe I'm really no good." Everyone who ever gets on a stage, at least, always thinks they know what's going on in music. I started double-faking myself out, even to the point of really knowing what I wanted to do.

Early—you know, fourteen or fifteen. And getting sidetracked from the time I was about eighteen till I was about twenty-one, listening to all this crap and saying, "Yeah, yeah, I guess you're right." Throwing away everything I had taught myself to believe. "Yeah, I guess you're right." No one really knows what's gonna happen. No one really . . . it doesn't matter if you're good or not. It's just kinda luck. You gotta throw enough stuff against the walls and some of it sticks. Maybe you'll be the lucky one. (1970)

At the same time John Fogerty was learning to play his instruments, the other future members of Creedence Clearwater Revival were developing their own musical interests. While Fogerty remembers being the only one in the band who was into traditional "Americana," everyone shared the popular musical mix ranging from the pioneering rock and roll of Carl Perkins, Bo Diddley, Elvis Presley, and Chuck Berry through R & B hits by the Crows and Five Royales to the commercial blues of Jimmy Reed and Howlin' Wolf. While Fogerty often cited Ray Charles's In Person *as his favorite album, he paid close attention to guitarists such as Duane Eddy, Scotty Moore, and James Burton.*

Tom Fogerty

I could read music when I was seven years old and played the violin until I was eleven. By the time I was sixteen I knew all of the rock and roll chords on the piano and the open chords on guitar. (1985)

Stu Cook

Doug and I met in seventh grade and we were friends before we started the band together. We were social cutups in school. We were both in the same homeroom with [students whose last names began with] the letter

"C." We kinda took to each other, and then this music thing came up. I played piano, I played trumpet before that. Doug had no musical experience, no formal training. We just sort of all learned our stuff together. We're self-taught on our current instruments. (1998)

Doug Clifford

I remember starting to play drums. There was a game called Caroms. It was my brother's Christmas present, and he never got them out. So I took the Caroms sticks to wood shop and cut 'em in half and made drumsticks out of 'em. (Of course a week later my brother brought his buddies over to play Caroms and that was basically an ass-whipping for me.) I had a brass lamp in my bedroom, a silly little thing, a conelike lamp. I'd set my books up, and instead of doing homework I'd play the radio and tap around on the books and use the brass light as a cymbal, and that was the beginning of it.

I had a bass drum I'd borrowed from a neighbor; it was a marching bass drum. I bought a snare drum and balanced it on a flowerpot stand, one of those old fiberglass things that looks like a bullet head, fifties art, I guess. I took the pot out of it and it was a tripod that way, and I put my snare drum on top of that.

I ran into John Fogerty in junior high school. I was walking by the music room and I heard authentic Fats Domino piano and Little Richard stuff coming out of the music room, which was a sacrilege. So I knew Mrs. Stark wasn't around. There was a real skinny little kid in there, a white kid, playing this stuff. So I listened for a while. I was kinda the guy who MC'd everything. I was Mr. School Spirit, I was a real outgoing, gregarious kinda guy, and John was just the opposite. He was very quiet and timid and lacked self-confidence, but he sure could play.

So I listened for a while, and I boldly said, "Hey, that's original Fats

Domino and Little Richard note for note, do you wanna start a band?"
He said, "Yes, but actually I play guitar." So I said, "Do you have a piano
player?" He said, "I got two guys I'm gonna try out. I told them I would."
The guys that he mentioned were tough guys, kinda punks, what we
called greasers in those days. I just kinda went, "Oh man, I don't know
about hanging out with those guys." At any rate, needless to say, they
were flakes, they were out chasing girls or working on somebody else's
car. So I said, "Hey, my best friend's name is Stu Cook. He's got a piano
and a rumpus room and his dad's a rich lawyer and he's taking piano
lessons and he hates it. He has to play classical music. I bet he'd be
great."

That was like two months after John and I had started playing. I was
going over to his house and he was playing guitar and he'd come to my
house and vice versa. So I did buy a drum set, an old funky thing. I saved
my allowance and worked real hard. I was the gardener and the maid in
the house with both parents working, so that got me the allowance to buy
my drum set. John had a Silvertone guitar and amp that he got from
Sears. So we started teaching Stu the songs, and we were an instrumental trio called the Blue Velvets, and that was really the beginning of it, in
junior high school in the eighth grade. (1998)

John Fogerty

Around 1953, I started to notice the rhythm-and-blues songs by Bo
Diddley, Chuck Berry, and things like that. They appealed to me more
than other songs. From there it grew into different kinds of music. We
all sort of skipped over the Fabian type of music. First impressions were
the best and we stuck with that old stuff. Diddley and Carl Perkins made
me want to pick up a guitar. My main influence, my first influence, would
be the Memphis Sun Records kind of thing, that sound. Jerry Lee Lewis

didn't have that many hits, but his influence, nostalgically anyway, far surpasses what he actually did. Because he sort of cut out his own niche, and that's his own from now on. Carl Perkins, same thing. There'll never be another "Blue Suede Shoes." Even though he only made two records that were heard on the West Coast, I studied each note and lived with that for ten years. Two records that were popular—I don't know, I suppose he had lots of them, there were only two of them out here. Until about 1961, [when] we got another one— I think it was called "Pointed Toed Shoes." The first Elvis Presley album [is one of my favorites] because it's uncitified. It's all really honest music. It didn't have a lot of extra stuff like vocal choruses and orchestras. That's lasted through the years for me. (1969, 1970)

Among guitarists, Duane Eddy was the real thing. Certainly I was influenced by Scotty Moore and James Burton. I think everybody has to say that. They were there making hot records with great solos on them all the time. I mean, Elvis made it and all that, but something came with him besides a voice. That was that great guitar. I have no idea what some of that stuff would sound like without Scotty Moore playing—you know, with some real country guitar. His style was very individualized. "Bad Moon Rising" has a riff that's vintage Scotty. I didn't know until much later that James Burton played on Dale Hawkins's "Suzie Q." That's a heck of a record. But the Ricky Nelson stuff, like the solo in "Believe What You Say," was just so mind-boggling. That's like hearing Hendrix for the first time; it was a new tone—and it was so high. Records were still kind of dull and limited in the high end then. That record still sounds great. Everybody always mentions rockabilly, and they forget that Ricky Nelson and his band were one of rockabilly's finest. So I'd say those two, and the Ventures, Duane Eddy—and any time there was a solo by some obscure group, like "Torquay" by the Fireballs. I remember the solo on the Five Royales' record called "Slummer the Slum," which was just nasty. I bought that record and played it over and over. But blues guys, I never knew who they were. It was kind of a shade—or an attitude—that you drew from. I knew who Pop Staples was. I used to listen to a lot of gospel albums just because it sounded like the stuff I liked. I wasn't really into the message too much. Charlie Christian was an influence just for musicality. One of my favorite songs of all time is "Flying Home." I'd play that sucker over and over. To my ear, every jazz guitarist since Charlie Christian plays like him. They all play sax lines on guitar. (1985)

White kids started liking black music. There'd always been black music, but it was only played on the black stations locally. All of a sudden life started imitating art. In singles, there was a record called "Gee" by the Crows, and historically it's supposed to be the first. Then "Sh-Boom" by The Chords and "Earth Angel" by the Penguins. The beginnings. "Sh-Boom" seemed like blatant sex! One thing for sure: Every kid who picks up a guitar starts with "Honky Tonk." That was the best single. For longevity, the first Bo Diddley album had my interest. It has "I'm a Man," "Hush Your Mouth," "Before You Accuse Me," "Bo Diddley," and a few more. I like eleven out of the twelve tunes and those eleven were all in the same key. There's a lot of good guitar and singing. A little later on there came an album called *In Person* by Ray Charles— "Drown in My Own Tears" from that album is the definitive rock song of all time. It's just dripping with soul. And "Tell the Truth." That's probably the best live album ever made. Even though the music is very simple, the addition of that in-person echo and the audience reaction is incredible. Of all the albums I've had, this is probably my favorite. The musicians, the singing, the recording, everything is really together. (1969)

During the fifties, the blues were just another part of the exciting musical mix

26

being broadcast into El Cerrito. In later years, Fogerty would think back on what they meant to him at the time.

John Fogerty

The blues came to me because people were having hit records. They were on the R & B radio. In the early fifties that's what I heard. When you're six years old you're not researching in the library or going through the bins at the record store. And I dare say if there was a record store anywhere near where I lived, which there wasn't, they did not have any Muddy Waters, that's for sure. The only records for miles around were in the furniture store. When I studied more about race music and race records, I learned that was a very common connection, because the record player was a piece of furniture. So they sold the records where you could buy the piece of furniture. In the middle fifties, eventually you could get rock-and-roll records because that's what would sell. Kids would go there. I'd imagine in 1954 and '55 they were selling Patti Page and Tony Bennett, that sort of thing. Not a big selection either. I doubt there were more than fifty different titles, including the albums they had. I heard R & B on the radio. I never bought any of those records in that store. (1997)

Tom Fogerty

Melancholy deals with sophisticated love, whereas blues just has the pure physical emotional love. Just plain "she left me." The ghetto blues, if a guy's woman really loves him, that's his whole world. The only thing he had was her and if she leaves then it's all over. A melancholy song might be, "Well, my girl's leaving me, but I've at least got some bread and I'll find another chick somehow." There's a line there, but it's not simply money that makes it different.

It's a way of life that's different. . . . You can sense the depth in Howlin' Wolf's blues. He's paid a few dues. I get the feeling from Wolf's music that if he took his shirt off, he'd have scars on his back. He pulls all my sympathy out. [I heard him on] KWBR, especially "Smokestack Lightnin'." Was it "Moanin' in the Moonlight" or something? He's the one I can't remember the titles as much as with anyone else. I don't know why. Maybe because all the songs—I go back now and I hear them—are very similar. A lot of them are the same. "Spoonful," but that was much later. That was about 1962 or so that I heard that, and it was a shock.

Sophisticated music is musical blues because it's got a nobody-really-lives-in-ivory-towers kind of feeling. Everybody likes to see it on the screen, but when you got the blues you're not thinking, yeah, this is the part Clark Gable played in that movie. When you feel bad, you feel bad for you and you can identify a lot easier with B. B. King than Clark Gable. That whole trip, the thirties and Cole Porter, they really did it on a level of the white man seeing the black blues kind of thing. I could just picture this cat at the piano in a tuxedo writing a tune and his hair's in place and everything. But it's not just black people. White people are making a huge culture out of black blues now. Even the Irish situation now in Ireland. Anywhere you'll find the downtrodden, the outcasts, the ghettos. They're the ones who sing with that kind of emotion. They're in a situation that they can't do anything about and it comes out in their music. We're all human beings, all promiscuous, all steal, all get robbed. Same frustrations, so they sing about the same thing. The imagery might be different, the language or the words—but they feel the same things. Even the medieval English ballads. But you always can find humor in it, which is beautiful. Especially black blues. I don't pretend to be a professor studying the situation: "Aha—here we have a tribal gathering." I only know what I lived. It wasn't terrible at all for me. I've never starved for two weeks. My hardships are mental. It's really the same thing to be hung up in your head. That's why I can identify with black blues. Then, of course, you have someone really slick come along and play so-called blues. It's easy to distinguish between good and bad blues. (1970)

John Fogerty

I was on a blues kick at seven. When I started listening to radio in 1953, there was no pop station in our area. All we had was R & B. We just all got into that very early in life. And today, our music bears this trademark. It's not that we're a blues group. I don't think that's true at all. But I think many good things in music come from the blues roots. I listened to real blues first, like Howlin' Wolf. Even Clyde McPhatter with the Drifters was rhythm and blues. Then Chubby Checker came along. Now c'mon. There's a big difference between Wolf and Chubby. Blues isn't just notes. It's a whole sound and culture. Like fuzz and wah-wah are just faddy things. Nothing to do with blues. In five years we'll be saying, "Hey, remember those wah-wah pedals?"

Blues, we're trying to call it a music. That's like trying to call America a race. It's scattered. There's a blue feeling that comes from the blue devils. I've got the bad spirits, I've got the blue devils, I got the blues. Everybody feels them and each culture puts it out in a certain way. I think the same kind of sad and happy at the same time. Not that "I'm happy to be sad" kind of thing. It's more like "I'm sad and I'm gonna talk about that and maybe it'll make me feel good."

All the really great records or people who made them somehow came from Memphis or Louisiana or somewhere along the Mississippi River in between. I just had a lifelong dream that I wanted to live there. I never even thought about social pressures. To me, it just represented something earlier, like 1807, before computers and machinery complicated everything, when things were calm and relaxed. And singers like Howlin' Wolf and Muddy Waters gave me the feeling that they were right there, standing by the river. Carl Perkins, the first one who ever made me think about being a musician and a singer, made his greatest records right there by the river in Memphis. I really enjoyed the whole Southern folk legend . . . Mark Twain, Tom Sawyer, Huck Finn, the river, and all that went with it. That river and the South just seem to be where all the music that's kicked everything off started from or sounds like. (1970)

I grew up with the blues. This was not like I'd just come from Tibet or Mars. But I was doing it from afar. I was listening to the blues as a fan, the records were all I had to go on. I barely knew anything about Muddy Waters's real life. I knew he had this great band, you hear those things. I knew about his outbreak in Chicago. Those guys down on Maxwell Street [in Chicago], like Little Walter, everybody was plugged in. It's awesome. So that's pretty important, that's something I really didn't know or appreciate when I was a kid. But I did appreciate the fire on those records. (1997)

GOLLIWOGS

T he myth of the garage-band-made-good was in place before anyone had heard of Creedence Clearwater Revival. That included the members of the band, who served their apprenticeships in groups whose names trace the changing currents of rock-and-roll fashion from the late fifties to the mid sixties: the Playboys, Spyder Webb and the Insects, Tommy Fogerty and the Blue Velvets, the Visions, and the Golliwogs, a name bestowed by Fantasy Records executives mesmerized by the British Invasion. At one point, a typographical error transformed the group into the Blue Violets, anticipating the advent of Flower Power by a half decade.

Whatever the band might have been called on the mimeographed posters advertising its appearances at teen clubs, roadhouses, drunken frat parties, and military bases, the group had embarked on its journey down the long road described in "Lodi" (where, in true mythic fashion, no version of the group ever actually played). Lodi represented a typical stop on the central California rock-and-roll circuit where, as John Fogerty remembered, the still-underage group played for "fifty dollars and all the beer we could drink." "I think we were in it for the beer," he recalled. One irony of "Lodi," as Dave Marsh points out, is that

Fogerty's lyrics bemoan the fact that he's spent a whole year on the road without making the big time. In fact, CCR's apprenticeship lasted almost exactly a decade.

It began in 1958 when John Fogerty, Stu Cook, and Doug Clifford formed a garage band with John on guitar, Stu on piano, and Doug banging away at the old snare drum propped up on a flowerpot. The same year, Tom Fogerty joined the Playboys, with whom he sang and played several instruments. It wasn't until 1968, when "Suzie Q" made the national charts, that all the hard work started to pay off. In between, the group made its recording debut backing up a black doo-wop singer; released nearly a dozen forgettable singles, including the medium-sized regional hit "Brown-Eyed Girl" (not to be confused with the Van Morrison classic); and began its fateful association with Fantasy and Saul Zaentz. Stu Cook earned his college degree; Tom Fogerty started a family and pursued a career at Pacific Gas & Electric; the draft board found John Fogerty and Doug Clifford, who both avoided Vietnam by, in Fogerty's phrase, "finagling" their way into reserve units.

All the while, John Fogerty's musical vision was developing from what he called "thin, white rock and roll" to something closer to the Southern voices that still resonated in his mind. He'd discovered his singing voice during a short-term gig with a pickup band in Portland, Oregon, where he was checking out the Northwest rock scene centered on Paul Revere and the Raiders. Although Tom Fogerty claimed his brother's estimates that he'd spent four thousand hours in the studio were probably inflated, John clearly put in enough hours to learn what he needed to know when he got the chance to produce CCR.

But ultimately "Lodi" has it right. Fogerty's Golliwogs found their voices and shaped their myth on the roads of northern and central California, during the endless hours playing for drunken crowds who wanted another round of "Hully Gully," "Walk Don't Run," "Green Onions," and "Louie Louie." By the time John Fogerty and Doug Clifford came off active duty in 1967, the group was ready to change its name and give substance to its dream.

John Fogerty

We were just your basic American garage band of the really early sixties. So I was going on what I saw in the world. I didn't really pull out what was inside me yet. Basically we were a garage band, a little band. We didn't think of ourselves as a little band though. You have these illusions in your mind even though you're in the eighth grade or ninth grade. But in those days the hot bands or the role models were people like the Ventures, Duane Eddy, Johnny and the Hurricanes. We were a three-piece instrumental band, and I wrote lots of instrumentals for the band. I played lead guitar. So I wasn't writing any songs with lyrics, and I wasn't delving into that whole thing that was lurking inside of me at all, except maybe a few of the titles of songs that I had in those days. Even stylistically, the music was pretty much three white boys from a middle-class suburb, and we played kind of thin, white rock and roll without a lot of string-bending and not a lot of grease at all. The kind of stuff that is so popular now with alternative bands. (1997)

We were all on the same wavelength, really. I just had to decide whether I would join [Stu and

John Fogerty, guitarist *(Courtesy Graham Niven)*

Doug's] band or they would join mine. I chose the latter. And once we got started we were literally the only group playing in school. We were playing blues, not rock and roll, but most of [the kids] didn't understand what we were talking about musically. They didn't know the difference. When we started, we had the greasy hair and ducktails and the matching outfits. We were trying to be like the Viscounts and the Wailers. You know, a "teen band." We got together in 1959 and made a record the same year, backing up a black singer from Richmond, James Powell, on Christy Records. It was actually played on the radio here—"Beverly Angel." (1969, 1985)

Doug Clifford

Tom would come to some of our gigs. We weren't very good, so he was kind of our special guest star. He was the singer in another band called Spyder Webb and the Insects, and they were greasers and he wasn't. Tom was the one early on who had the vision of having the record career. It wasn't John, it was Tom. He invited us because he couldn't get the guys in his band to come to a recording session 'cause they weren't getting paid and there were no chicks there. So he asked if we'd back him up and we did and then it was Tommy Fogerty and the Blue Velvets. We cut a bunch of records and started learning our way around in a studio and focusing in on the idea that one day we'd be able to have songs on the radio and be stars like the idols that we saw growing up on *Bandstand* and shows like that. (1998)

Tom Fogerty

As Tommy Fogerty, I joined my first band, the Playboys, in 1958, as lead singer and part-time piano and guitar player. I was sixteen years old and a junior at St. Mary's—Berkeley High School. In early 1959, I joined a much better band, Spyder Webb and the Insects, and we landed a record contract with Del-Fi Records in Hollywood, hoping to fill the shoes of Richie Valens, who had just died in a plane crash with Buddy Holly and the Big Bopper. In June 1959, I had a diploma in one hand, a record contract in the other. Unfortunately, that first record at Del-Fi never happened and the song "Lyda Jane" was lost in the shuffle. (1985)

I went to Hollywood in '59 and I stayed two weeks. I had some tapes under my arm. They all said, "Get lost." In those days, it was coffeehouses on the Strip, as opposed to head shops. Yeah, I saw the gay producers, the old men after the kids. I sized up the whole scene, mentally, and I came home. Tapes under my arm. I waited to come back to Hollywood until we were Creedence Clearwater Revival. So now I can look up at that street sign that says Hollywood and Vine, and instead of hating it, like I did, I can say, "OK, street sign, I just got top billing at the Hollywood Bowl." It is the only way to come back to Hollywood. (1971)

The Insects broke up, and in November 1959 I joined forces with my brother as Tommy Fogerty and the Blue Velvets. The Blue Velvets were an instrumental trio. The other guys were all fourteen years old and went to the same junior high school. We were determined to make it, and after rejections by many U.S. record companies, I landed my second record contract with Wayne Farlow of Orchestra Records in San Francisco. The Blue Velvets were too young to sign a legal contract, but we had a verbal agreement for twenty-five percent each and credit on the record label. Contrary to popular belief, the Blue Velvets were the backup band on my records. I was under contract as a singer and I also produced the records we made during the years 1959–63. The first Tommy Fogerty and the Blue Velvets' record, "Come On Baby," backed with "Oh My Love," didn't get played, but Casey Kasem at KEWB in Oakland told me to hang in there. Casey was program director at the time, and when the second record came out, they jumped on it. "Have You Ever Been Lonely?" backed with "Bonita," was somewhat of a local hit. The third record, "Now You're Not Mine," backed with "Yes You Did," came out with a printing error on the label, "Tommy Fogerty and the Blue Violets." This record died and I decided to wait out my option with the record company because they didn't have national distribution. (1985)

John Fogerty

The first thing we played for was sock hops at Portola Junior High School. That was about four months. Doug and I had been together since April; we got Stu in September, I think, of '59, and we played at the school at the end of September or the first of October. And we played a Boys' Club thing right at the end of '59. And then the next summer we went around to all the country fairs, representing El Cerrito Boys' Club. For years we never played within one hundred miles of our homes. We were getting up to fifty dollars a night and all the beer we could drink. I think we were in it for the beer.

People looked at us like we were the Four Puppets. Everybody wants either a fast or a slow number but nobody cares if it's a blues or a polka. I just got used to it. Those frat parties were such drunken orgies, anyway, that they didn't care whether we had a mike or not. They just wanted the music to sing along with.

We had ninety percent original material when we first formed the group. Mostly instrumentals. There wasn't much happening lyrically in those days. We learned instrumentals off of albums that nobody knew. We also did "Bulldog" and "Rawhide." We could never find records that had parts we wanted to play. So we wrote our own stuff. The instrumentals were all the same—sort of Duane Eddy-ish. When "Pipeline" came along, we played it as a copout. We had nothing else to play. We did it tongue in cheek. That little riff that fumbles down with a hollow sound. (1969, 1970)

We were pretty much your average punk, white garage band. We were a high school rock-and-roll band, a very typical American band. A little bit of Ventures, "Wipe Out," "Louie Louie," right down the rock-and-roll line. We weren't heavily off into James Brown any more than most white high school kids would have known. We weren't Delta relics at all. That was not even in our consciousness at the time. We did "Midnight Hour," everybody did. We never really did "Mustang Sally," but everybody else did. For some reason we just skipped that one. But going way back to when we were in ninth grade, we did "Hully Gully." And we also used to do "Annie Had a Baby" 'cause we thought we were really gettin' down.

I remember playing for a high school reunion. It was actually our high school, but it was from ten years before us. So it was the class of fifty-three and this was about 1963, and we were still in high school. We did "Green Onions" and this black guy came up. His name was R. B. King, and that would have made him about twenty-eight years old or so. And he says, "You boys do that rock and roll pretty good. But there's this little in-between you're missing." He was trying to compliment us. But he was also trying to say "when you do 'Green Onions' there's this in-between that you're missin'" And later he would have said "soul." And it's absolutely the truth, because I've been around all kinds of musicians. I mean, we were high school kids, we didn't have that. We couldn't play a shuffle to save our lives, anyway. It's something most white people can't do. It's almost a joke. The black guys would sit there and shuffle to death playing "Honky Tonk" or "Green Onions." I know now exactly what he was talking about, but I was about seventeen at the time of that little speech he made: "There's that in-between you're missing that when you get that then you'll have that 'Green Onions' down." I thought about that a lot over the years. (1997)

I did play with other people during that time, of course, but from the first day of the Blue Velvets, I always thought of that as the group. They went off to college, and I still thought, "No, this is the real group. We'll get back together eventually." (1985)

I was doing some work in the studio, at Sierra Sound in Berkeley. There was a time, around eleventh or twelfth grade, when all three of us—Doug, Stu, and I—were going there on Sunday afternoons, just making tracks, messing with tape recorders. The owner, Bob DiSousa, was equally interested, because everybody's dream is to make a hit record. Around that time, Bob started using me on little sessions that were happening. He'd need some Floyd Cramer piano or Cropper-style guitar, and he'd call me. I did dozens of sessions. But from day one, I also wanted to know what made this sound this way, how he got things down on tape. I had a concern about the overall, because the more you know, the better off you're going to be. (1985)

Doug Clifford

We only knew so many songs, so we'd play the same songs over again and tell the audience we had a special request. We had just run out of songs to play. One of the ways John developed when we played as a trio was that we didn't have a PA system. So he sang over the band and that really developed the power in his voice. (1997)

Tom Fogerty

We always envisioned a rock band like the Crickets. Two guitars, bass, and drums. Just bottom, drums, rhythm, and lead. We'd just finish a great song of our own and somebody would come up and ask if we knew "Wipe Out." First we'd say "no" as a joke. We played a lot of drunken frat parties and it was amazing how many people were digging it, because we were just laughing at it. We weren't all that great at the time, but we threw in mistakes on purpose— change the drumbeat and play it too fast or slow. It was really nonsense, that kind of music. (1970)

During 1964, while other members of the group were attending to school, jobs, and family concerns, John went to Portland, Oregon, for a short-term engagement with what amounted to a pickup band. It was there that he began to discover his singing voice.

John Fogerty

One of the reasons it took so long for Creedence to get anywhere is that everybody was off in different directions doing other things. Tom had a job and a family and that kind of thing, so it was hard for him to give that up. Stu was in school with the hatchet over his head by his father, you know, that kind of thing. Doug really wasn't quite sure yet, he was in school or he wasn't in school, that kind of thing.

So I went to Portland because I just wanted to play, that's all. It wasn't like I was leaving the group, at *all*. We had already recorded the record for Fantasy. There was no question that the Blue Velvets or the Golliwogs or whatever were the only group I was going to be with. This was just like a sabbatical to keep going. A guy I'd met in another group, he was calling himself the Apostles, a guy named Mike Byrnes and another guy named Tom Fanning. Portland was big on Paul Revere and that stuff then. They were preceding San Francisco as a gathering place for groups. A lot of groups were coming out of the Northwest, so we said, "Sure, let's go up to Portland and get something together." We found a bass player somewhere and a drummer up there, and got a job in a club for two weeks, and played for the Peace Corps once. Typical club job. We wanted to come home after three nights of it. It was a six-night-a-week, five-set-a-night kind of thing.

Well, one day I said, "I'm going to sing." And since I was out of my hometown, away from my parents and any of my friends, I kind of just told myself to go ahead and try it, don't be shy. I had taken a reel-to-reel tape recorder up there. I would record whole sets. Then I'd stay up until sunrise listening to myself. And I heard myself improve. I'd try something like a scream or a hard-edged "Well!" I'd hear myself try to do it on the tape, and the next night I'd go back and try something else. As I used to say, I developed a scream in Portland. (1993)

My singing doesn't have one source. I'd certainly have to tip my hat to Little Richard. But it's sort of a composite guy, because I love Wilson Pickett, and there are a few guys who have that sort of high, edgy thing, Little Richard being the best and the most famous. Wilson even screamed in tune. My voice came out a certain way, and I've learned to be that way. But it *is* an affectation; it's something I had to work on. That's the part that people don't understand. It's just like guitar playing. You decide in your mind that you want to get good, want to play. But it takes work and practice. . . . You end up getting to where you want, if you put in enough practice time. It was the same for me and my singing. I had a mental image of what my voice ought to sound like, but it sure didn't sound like that when I was fourteen— just kind of like any other kid whose voice was cracking. (1997)

Creedence Clearwater Revival's association with Fantasy Records, a jazz label then located in San Francisco, began in 1964, after the group watched a PBS special, The Anatomy of a Hit, *which focused on the Vince Guaraldi Trio's* "Cast Your Fate to the Wind," *which Fantasy released. John and Tom got in touch with Fantasy owners Sol and Max Weiss, who signed them to a contract and convinced them to change their name. Although the group decided on the Visions, Max Weiss used the Golliwogs, to try to cash in on the British Invasion. Meanwhile, Doug and Stu enrolled at San Jose State College and John worked as a shipping clerk at Fantasy, where he met Bay Area keyboardist Merl Saunders.*

John Fogerty

We saw *The Anatomy of a Hit* on Channel Nine. We'd been in and out of Sierra Sound and Music City and we had four instrumentals, two of which were mostly piano melodies. And at that point, as far as we were concerned, Vince seemed to hit a peak and then nothing happened, and we thought, "Wow! Maybe he could use our stuff." Everyone thinks that, right? And [the demos] were professionally done . . . like, I still like the tunes. Anyway, we saw Max and Sol Weiss on there. And we thought, "Wow! At least there's one record company in San Francisco. Let's try them." And we went over there with the idea of "sell the instrumentals." . . . Max convinced us that instrumentals weren't the thing, which wasn't our thing anyway, but we were tryin' to sell them for Vince. It got us in the door. He said, "Well, you should do vocals." Which is what we'd been doing all along. (1970)

Merl Saunders

I first met John back in 1963 when he was working in the shipping department at Fantasy. Fantasy was in this little place that was mostly a jazz label, and they kept all the boxes of records in this one room, just stacks and stacks of records. I'd just signed my first contract with Fantasy, and so I'd go into the shipping department and talk to the guys, and they'd go get copies of the albums for me. The Weisses owned Fantasy at the time. Saul Zaentz was in promotions back then. He bought the label four or five years later. When I started knowing them, they were called the Golliwogs. Their records were okay. (1998)

Tom Fogerty

Since we had decided to become a quartet, we opted to change the name to something more unified. Tommy Fogerty and the Blue Velvets were to become the Visions. Unfortunately, Max owned the company and stuck that name, the Golliwogs, on the label of our first single. We should have walked out on the spot. We always hated the name (I still do), but we wanted to make records and, like I said, it was Max's company. (1971)

John Fogerty

So we made, like, a dumb tape, a demonstration thing . . . down in that lean-to in the back. It was just supposed to be a demonstration. It was cut at seven and a half, like a home tape recorder, and we added a few things. Then I went off to Portland, and nine months later the record came out. Tom went over there every single day. We were convinced by this time that Jesse James or somebody'd gotten on the plane and stolen the tapes, and that was it. Anyway, nine months later, just before Christmas, the first single came out . . . the one that we'd recorded. We rushed over there, and we were all excited, and we listened to it. And we didn't look at it till, oh, a half hour later, we looked at the label, and it said "the Golliwogs." And we just, I don't know how to describe it because now I'm over it, but for four years it was like a nightmare. You know, I told myself, "It's okay, I like it. Yeah, it's okay, it's okay, I like it." And I knew

I didn't like it. And I couldn't face Doug and Stu because they were like, phew! Me and Tom told 'em, "Well, it's the only way we'll ever have a record out." But we didn't like it at all. For four years after that we were laughed at. You know, we were ashamed to say the name even. They'd ask us, "What's the name of your group?" And we'd turn the other way and say, "the Golliwogs." That kind of thing. (1970)

All the while, the real center of the group's musical life was the gigs in Bay Area clubs like the Monkey Inn and anonymous roadhouses such as the one immortalized in "Lodi."

Stu Cook

We played Sacramento to Yuba City, Marysville. I don't think we actually played Lodi, Doug thinks we did, but we played every other damn little town. Doug remembers an incident where we almost got our asses kicked in one bar. It was all part of the Central Valley, the San Joaquin valley experience. It coulda been any town. (1998)

John Fogerty

We never did play in Lodi. That was a title I'd had in my mind since I was about twelve or thirteen. I thought it would be cool to have a song called Lodi. But it was very representative geographically. I could picture what it was I was trying to say happening in Lodi. Especially when we were Golliwogs, we played all kinds of venues in northern California and central California, places like Modesto and Fresno that aren't quite south. We played all up and down the state and mostly in the middle of the state, Sacramento, Marysville, Roseville, those places. We played all kinds of one-nighters under less than glorious circumstances, a typical roadhouse band where you unload all the band's equipment out of the back of a VW microbus and saunter in and plug in to the club and the first thing the guy who owns the place says is, "Don't play loud."

The crowds were mostly younger people. Most of the time the places that would book the Golliwogs were not grizzled old Hell's Angels biker bars with forty-five-year-old tattoo guys. They were mostly younger places. We used to joke that Thursday night was divorcee night. There were women that were probably twenty-five but already divorced, and we used to joke that Thursdays were the nights all the women would show up looking for a date. But they ended up just sitting around talking to each other about how bad those men are. They've got the knowledge and the experience of the world and they were twenty-five years old, not much older than we were. (1998)

Doug Clifford

Stu and I were going to San Jose State and we'd drive up to Sacramento on the weekends. If it was a weekend where I had duty for the Coast Guard, I'd have to drive all the way back to San Jose, do my Saturday, drive out Saturday night and play, drive back Sunday, do all day Sunday, and try to go to class on Monday. We'd meet Tom and John or, when I got a VW bus, we'd pick them up and carry all the gear. We'd meet them and head off together. Later on, after we got out of school, we had a place out in the country in El Sobrante. Stu and I had a house where we could rehearse so we wouldn't disturb people in town. We kept our gear there and my bus and they'd drive out there. We called it the Shire. They'd meet us there and we'd drive off to gigs. It was a lot easier when I wasn't in school. (1998)

John Fogerty

We used the Monkey Inn, this beer bar in Berkeley where the owner showed horror movies every Monday night, as a coming-out period, as a breakout for us as entertainers. We had been doing frat parties and all that, but it wasn't until just before the Monkey Inn period that I started singing. I was about eighteen when we first got our introduction at the Monkey. We didn't know any of the people who went there. It was such a gross place—the people either made me laugh or sometimes disgusted me, so I usually wound up looking at the wall while I was singing. The wall would have all sorts of things written all over it, and I'd read it all. Then about once a month the owner would paint the wall and people would write all over it again. Looking at the wall got me in the habit of singing sideways and I used to drive soundmen crazy—"Sing straight into the mike!" No, I sing sideways. (1970)

The Monkey Inn gig evolved as early as 1964, after I went up to Portland. We came back to California, and one of the guys in that band re-formed essentially that same group and called it the Apostles. I was the guitar player, Doug was the drummer, and two other guys were playing keyboard or guitar. He got the gig at the Monkey Inn. It's on Ashby Avenue in Berkeley just across the line from Oakland. I remember that because when the Free Speech Movement started, a demonstration march came marching up Ashby Avenue and the police made them stop right at the line, which was about one block from the door. We played in the club, but the stage was on the wall where the door opened to the sidewalk. So Doug's rear end was sitting literally in the doorway and people could walk by when they had the door open and see the drummer. So this crowd that was on the radio and the TV news was being stopped a half a block away at the line, but they could hear the music coming out of this joint and that was us.

Some time went on and the band evolved. I got my guys in there. I got Tom and Stu and Doug playing the steady gig rather than that other band. Tom didn't really play guitar at the time. He just played tambourine.

We did play a few air force bases when we were the Golliwogs. We didn't have that repertoire yet. It was brutal. Man, that was a tough audience. Your musicianship, they're really looking at you. In those days, we couldn't cut it. (1997, 1998)

The group's first taste of success came in early 1966 when their "Brown-Eyed Girl," released on Fantasy's Scorpio Records subsidiary, became a regional hit, eventually selling ten to fifteen thousand copies. Two follow-up singles, "Fight Fire" and "Walking on the Water," failed to garner even that much attention.

Tom Fogerty

In and about February of 1964, three changes took place in the evolution of the band. First, the band became a quartet. All four of us should be considered founding members. Second, John and I formed a partnership as songwriters, using the pseudonyms Rann Wild and Toby Green (I was Wild, John was Green). Third, I signed my third recording contract— John, Doug, and Stu were still too young— this time with Max Weiss, one of the owners of Fantasy Records. The Golliwogs made seven singles between July 1964 and November 1967. All of the songs were written by Rann Wild and Toby Green (together and separately, like Lennon-McCartney) with the exception of number seven, which was written by T. Spicebush Swallowtail. John and I traded off on singing the lead on the single and on some [other songs] sang the lead together. We coproduced all seven. "Brown-Eyed Girl" and "Walking on the Water" got us lots of gigs in the valleys of inland northern California. (1985)

Doug Clifford

We had a regional hit called "Brown-Eyed Girl," not Van Morrison's song. It was number one in San Jose. Stu and I were going to San Jose University at the time and that was cool. (1998)

John Fogerty

When I was eighteen or nineteen I did a lot of things on paper. One of our first well-done records was "Brown-Eyed Girl," and I remember making a long graph like a computer printout—where this would overlap to this—trying to make the aural picture, you might say. There are some moments there, like in "Brown-Eyed Girl," which is a pretty superficial song, there's a little bit of the tonal and chordal structure that became Creedence. Certainly my voice in an immature way, but it's a lot of earnestness about nothing. "Brown-Eyed Girl" was studio-conceived, you might say. We weren't able to play as well as the record, so it was hard for us to come up with a follow-up, to tell you the truth. The material wasn't flowing or anything like that. . . . Stu only knew three notes on the bass, Tom played one string on the guitar, and then I filled in all the other instruments, organ, stuff like that. In other words, we weren't what you call an in-person group, we were a studio group. I'd say we had better taste than someone like the Monkees that were a studio-conceived thing, too. But in person we weren't much more powerful than the Monkees. One voice and a drum just isn't enough to keep an interest going. I knew what I wanted in my head, but it was a matter of convincing the other guys that, "Hey, we can do it! So rehearse, learn your instrument." That kind of thing. (1970, 1985, 1997)

Tom Fogerty

In the middle of sixty-five, I realized John should be singing lead. I could sing, but he had a sound. Sure, there could be all sorts of problems

between John and me—but we're brothers. I worked a whole lot of straight jobs, but we always played music. And in sixty-seven we said, "We have to devote our whole lives to music or else it won't happen." Two or three months before our first album, we had exactly two dollars in our common checking account. OK. Doing this, right now, I have a hundred times more freedom than I ever could. What's an ego trip beside that? (1985)

John Fogerty

I knew I had potential . . . I knew it wasn't showing up very well. But even with the minor successes of "Brown-Eyed Girl" or something . . . just knowing that we were able to go into a room just like this, that just had a couple of microphones in it,

The original lead singer *(Courtesy Graham Niven)*

and make a record that *sounded* like a record. Someone should have figured out from that, "Hey! There's *somethin'* going on there." . . . I mean, we had a lot of things against us. We weren't ready either. I really admit that. If "Brown-Eyed Girl" had been a hit, we would have been like every other one-hit artist, we would have never gone back and really, you know, *really* tried to *really* make it tight. We would have just thought, hey, it's simple, and that would have been it. (1970)

In 1966, with Stu still attending San Jose State and Tom Fogerty supporting a family by working at Pacific Gas & Electric, John Fogerty and Doug Clifford received their draft notices. Both wound up joining the reserves, which required six months of active duty. They emerged from the army with a renewed sense of dedication to their music.

Stu Cook

We had made that decision before John and Doug went in [to the service]. As I recall, we played a gig at a little place called Mousey's at Davis, California. They went in, but before they went we all said when you guys get out, we're gonna really give this a shot. I was still at San Jose, going into my senior year. I remember having a 2S deferment. When I graduated, I was looking at going 1A, but I managed to work a 4F out of the draft board. I remember doing some cartwheels and running around screaming and freaking out about that. I don't have to go, ever, they're not taking me. (1998)

John Fogerty

I got drafted, but I was able to finagle my way into a reserve unit. So I went on active just for the six-month shot and then every summer for two weeks. But it was at the height of the war and all the rules were changing. There were National Guard guys worrying that their units would get shipped over to Vietnam. It was amazing. Things sort of got real altered, but luckily for me, I didn't have to go overseas or serve the full three years in the hard-core army, the regular army. I was at Fort Bragg, Fort Knox, and Fort Lee. (1997)

I managed to get in the reserves because I had contacted them before I got drafted. If I knew then what I know now, I never would've been involved. They couldn't see my hair this long, and I had to convince myself I was a slave. It was sixty-seven and sixty-eight. They still hadn't got used to hippies and communists. (1970)

Doug Clifford

And then the Vietnam thing was warming up. Stu was 4F and I was 1A. I was working my way through college, working from five in the afternoon till two in the morning as a janitor. I thought, if I take twelve hours and the grades are okay, the army won't bother me. Well, that was rather naive.

They came after me and I wound up going into the Coast Guard Reserve. There was a year and a half waiting list; a buddy of mine, big six-foot-four baseball player, got in on an athletic scholarship. So we lied and said I was a star football player in high school, four years all-city and I was playing freshman ball at San Jose State and going to play varsity the next year. The guy won't check up 'cause he'll take my word for it. I'm a little guy, one hundred and sixty pounds. I was a good athlete, but my parents gave me a choice of practicing my drums after school or going out for sports. So I took the drum practice, which was a tough decision for a kid who was a good athlete. They swore me into the Coast Guard Reserve that day. I'd already passed the army physical and had my notice of acceptability; I was going in and so they swore me in on the spot.

I started feeling guilty that I took some guy's place, so I worked out for two months—I was pretty fast for a guy who didn't train. So I went in and played in this football league. Most of these guys were college football players who just didn't make grades. We were really good; I made first-string defensive back and suicide man on all special teams. We were undefeated, and I think my record for interceptions still holds—I averaged, like, two a game in a ten-game season. It was my speed made that happen. So there I was in the reserves. I wound up going on a starvation diet to get out. I had sideburns that they allowed me to grow, and then the company commander panicked. He was a little guy with a Napoleon complex and went after me. So I had to starve myself to say I was psyched out that they were trying to take my music away. It was a hard thing to do. I'd eat every fifteen minutes like a hummingbird. But I had to say I was sick, and they let me out with an honorable, and that was right about when the band was starting to break, right before we were starting to have hit records. (1998)

John Fogerty

You're marching all day long in hundred-degree heat on the pavement and you have a lot of time to think. Just endless plodding around, they don't know what to do with you. So I would see my spit-shined shoes—you always had to have the toes like glass, real shiny—and I would be seeing this shiny toe with one spot and it would move over. I mean, that's how delirious you are in that heat. And the other part of the time I was writing a song which became "Porterville." I realized while I was doing it, in the army with no instruments, no connection, I was not even in the outside world, but somehow this was better. Something had happened to me and I resolved at that point to not be mediocre, to write real songs. (1997)

By the time I got out of the army, it was like, now we have to learn to grow, kind of like in the old vaudeville sense, so that when we got out on the road we could convince 'em, knock 'em dead. I don't care if we're playing somebody else's song, if we just play the jukebox songs. It doesn't have to be our song; that approach is all wrong. We have to be able to play music first. I got back, my head was straight again. . . . When I was, say, fourteen or fifteen, and somewhere in between then and being twenty I got too self-conscious of things, too aware, like, "Oh, do I fit here? Do I fit there?" You know, too analytical, that whole thing. And you get all tied up in knots, I guess. What happened to start *us* off, I think . . . a little, maybe a *lot* of luck. . . . But mainly just me deciding, well, you know, don't get all involved with analyzing everything and worrying about infinitesimal little points, just go on straight ahead. . . . The difference to, say, a year previous, was, finally, we were sure of ourselves. We had a repertoire, were able to do it well; and we had, I guess, whatever presence you need. We were just happy with what we were doing. Before we were always so critical. We had so many things in the way. We never had a PA that worked! No one seemed to understand that, you know, you need a good PA system! (1970)

After John and Doug came off active duty in July 1967, three things happened that were to prove crucial to the group's success. First, all four members made primary commitments to music, which allowed them to establish their reputation as one of the best northern California rock bands. Stu and Doug rented a house that served as the band's headquarters, and the band bought a VW minibus, although they lacked the funds to paint over the name of the previous owner, the "Du-All Paint Company." Second, Saul Zaentz, at that time on extremely cordial terms with everyone in the group, bought Fantasy Records. Third, they changed their name.

Tom Fogerty

In the summer of 1967, the Golliwogs, a.k.a. the Visions, dropped everything to become full-time musicians and a totally committed group, camaraderie personified. The band got into a groove of rehearsing every day and taking every gig we could get, total commitment. Stu Cook and I backed the band financially. I quit my job at PG&E and put up my entire life savings, one thousand two hundred and fifty dollars, and Stu matched it by selling his car. Stu became the soundman. Doug had an old Volkswagen bus and was put in charge of transportation. John had the guitar that Stu found for him while John was putting in his six months in the army reserve, early in 1967. At that time, I was playing rhythm guitar and managing all the band's business. I used to give everyone twenty dollars per week to live on—twenty dollars per week. For the first ten years of the band, I was the manager and sang a lot of the lead. It's a matter of record that I took care of all the real business of running the band: record contracts, bookings, union dues, phone calls, letters, collecting and distributing money. . . . [When the band became the Golliwogs] I was the oldest member of the group, twenty-two at the time, and no one else could legally sign a contract. These things I did eagerly from November 1959 through January 1969, the first ten years of the band. (1985)

Stu Cook

Everybody quit what else they were doing. Tom quit work, John and Doug struggled to get out of the army, and we did it full-time. We worked every night and we practiced every day and it took us one year. (1997)

Tom Fogerty

I worked a whole lot of straight jobs—I drove a truck, [worked at] gas stations, a steel mill in Oakland, a utility company—six years there. But we always played music, and in 1967 we said, "We have to devote our whole lives to music or else it won't happen."

I worked at PG&E during that time, and on Saturdays John and I would drive over to San Francisco to have lunch with Max and, quite often, Saul Zaentz. Saul was national sales manager at Fantasy and showed much optimism about our records. One day I looked at myself in the mirror—literally; I was fixing my tie on my way to my eight-to-five job—and I saw that just because I wasn't in high school didn't mean I couldn't continue with my music dream. I was doing something I didn't want to know, something I used to laugh at other people for. At that precise point, that morning, I turned. I've hated neckties ever since. Sounds like a movie, doesn't it? (1971)

Late in 1967, without telling the band, Max Weiss sold Fantasy Records. Saul Zaentz, who really liked us and our music, and a few friends, including Ralph Kaffel, [who has been] president of Fantasy since 1973, scraped together the money to buy the company. (1985)

John Fogerty

We knew Saul mostly as a friend. He worked there, he worked *for* Fantasy. I'm not really sure what he was doing—I think it was sales representative, but I never knew what those titles meant. But he was objective, you know. He wasn't worried about the record coming out. He just liked us [and] we liked him. Eventually I went to work there as a shipping clerk. So, like, I was working for the same company Saul was working for. And it was like that, mostly just good friends. And suddenly, in October, I guess of sixty-seven, we got a phone call from Saul saying, "I just bought Fantasy Records." And it was kind of weird, because I'd been telling the group all through the summer of sixty-seven—I just had this feeling—things were gonna kind of come to a head in October. And I kept saying, "Something great's gonna happen in October." And I didn't know what it was. I didn't even know if I was just giving 'em the Knute Rockne speech, you know! . . . There's this phone call, and we knew right away that it was momentous to us in our lives. Wow! 'Cause Saul was straight ahead! We knew what he was like. And he said, "I bought the company, and will you stay with it?" And we said, "Sure!"

From there it really picks up. [Saul] didn't have a lot of money, really. He had put up most of what he had, I guess, for the company. And he got some other people to be partners. But he made a personal loan for us to get one amplifier. And that was what we desperately needed—a lead guitar amp for me. We had no money. Not even the ghost of it. We asked him for a lot of things. We needed a van, we needed this, we needed that. But we said we can do without all of those, if we have to, but we *gotta* have an amp. And he said, "All right." And he went, and in his own name, not in the company name, he borrowed the money, and we got the amp. (1970)

Saul Zaentz

One of the things when we signed them was, I said I hated the name "Golliwogs." It was ridiculous—a stupid name. They played with big white hats, ridiculous. So they said, "What name do you want to give us?" I said, no, you come up with ten names, I'll come up with ten names and the first one we like we'll use. I still have this picture in my mind of the guys walking up the stairs, they said, "Okay, what's your first name?" I said, "No, tell me yours." Creedence Clearwater Revival. I just tore up my list. (1998)

John Fogerty

Creedence was the name of a friend of ours, believe it or not, and it also means "to believe in." With Clearwater, I got that thought from watching an Olympia Beer commercial, which shows the beautiful clear water they use for the beer. The idea really appealed to us because it seemed to symbolize the purity that we think is part of it all. With Revival, we feel there's excitement and fervor in the whole thought and, frankly, we like that idea. Clearwater was something deep, true, and pure, through which the light always shines. The most important part was Revival. I meant it as a personal resurgence within ourselves—we really needed it. (1969, 1970)

Tom Fogerty

One of the first things we did after Saul took over was change our name. Remember, the Golliwogs was Max's idea. We went to Saul and it was mutually agreed that we could and would change our name. Many names were thrown into the hat, including Deep Bottle Blue, Muddy Rabbit, Gossamer Wump, and Credence Nuball and the Ruby. Credence Nuball was a friend of a friend of mine and later came to the Fillmore to meet us. Anyway, to make a long story short, I came up with Creedence and John came up with Clearwater Revival. As 1968 became a reality, we were ready! We had our own new energy, an essentially new record company, and a whole batch of new songs. We were in the right place, San Francisco, at the right time. (1985)

John Fogerty

The name was better than we were when we finally decided on the name. We sort of at that point decided, "Well, now we've got to live up to the name." It's really a good name, rather than the Golliwogs or whatever. It sort of inspired us. I remember Buffalo Springfield or Jefferson Airplane were good names. There's an image you get, you know. And the same with Creedence Clearwater Revival. It was something we sort of said, "Well, we better really get together now." It was like we better be more polished than we had been. So we tried to give ourselves a lot more depth in our performance.

We knew we had lived with a bad name and told ourselves it was all right. And so it was twice the jump of coming from just average. But it really helped us. Gave us a higher esteem of what we were shooting for. That sounds pretty stuffy, but it just made everything fit together much better. . . . *Finally* we were a working band, and we had a real name. It was up to us to make that all mean something. (1970)

SAN FRANCISCO AND THE SWAMP

om Fogerty was right when he observed that Creedence Clearwater had been "in the right place, San Francisco, at the right time." CCR wasn't precisely a "San Francisco" band, at least not in the same sense as Jefferson Airplane, Moby Grape, Quicksilver Messenger Service, and the Grateful Dead. El Cerrito was across the Bay, closer to Berkeley than the Haight-Ashbury district where, as myth had it, the gentle people with flowers in their hair came in search of Aquarian love and chemical ecstasy. While CCR appreciated the vibrations, their approach to rock had been forged playing for beer drinkers in roadhouses where the jukebox was likely to mix in some Buck Owens and Merle Haggard with the Top Forty.

The members of CCR stayed pretty much clear of the Haight drug scene, even during its sunniest phase, and kept to the conservative side of the hippie fashion continuum. More important, Fogerty's developing musical vision placed a premium on hit singles. So it's not surprising that there were times when Fogerty felt like "an outsider in my hometown." It certainly didn't help matters any that Ralph Gleason's liner notes to CCR's first album relegated the group to the fringes of a scene that, he wrote, was revolutionizing American music. Gleason divided the San Francisco music scene into "three concentric circles" descending *from the gaudy heights of the major ballrooms where the Airplane and Dead played to small clubs like the Lion's Share, the New Monk, and Deno and Carlo's. Gleason didn't even mention the group he was ostensibly writing about until the final paragraph, when he admitted that they gave "every indication of keeping the strength of the San Francisco sound undiminished." In truth, CCR found its sound playing clubs Gleason probably would have ranked somewhere between circles eight and fourteen. "It was nice of him to mention us on our own album," Fogerty observed.*

Still, San Francisco was precisely the right place for CCR in 1968, when their version of "Suzie Q," a hit for Dale Hawkins in 1957, started receiving airplay on the pioneering underground radio station KMPX. KMPX and its successor, KSAN, provided a perfect outlet for the sound that soon would be instantly recognizable as "swamp rock." If CCR didn't really look like a San Francisco band, the bluesy guitar jams in "Suzie Q" certainly didn't alienate audiences who grooved to the Airplane, the Dead, or the Paul Butterfield Blues Band, which CCR played with once they'd made the jump from the roadhouses to the Fillmore West. The exposure on KMPX caught the attention of programmers in Chicago, initiating a string of hit singles that made CCR a constant presence in the top twenty for the next four years.

CCR's ambivalent relationship with San Francisco continued once "Proud Mary" propelled the group into the first rank of American rock bands. For one thing, the swamp rock sound that assumed classic form on the Bayou Country album tricked most listeners in the East and Midwest into thinking the group came from Louisiana or Mississippi. "Even people from Louisiana thought we were from Louisiana," Stu Cook recalled. On the other hand, Fogerty's sense of being an outsider diminished as CCR became better known. Although the group's bluesy lyrics rarely echoed the Haight's party line of peace, love, and understanding, the band lent its support to the counterculture. "Eventually, San Francisco kind of adopted us," Fogerty observed. A crucial moment in the adoption process came when CCR rallied to the support of KMPX DJs and workers when they went on strike.

John Fogerty

I felt that we had something to offer, and we were sort of adopted. They were playing "Suzie Q," and they were probably playing it eight times a day, they really liked it even though it was eight minutes long, or maybe that's why, gives the DJ a chance to take a break. They embraced us right away. When the first album came out with "Suzie Q" and "I Put a Spell on You," that's where we went. I took it to the station and did an interview with a guy named Tony Pig. It came out on my birthday, so that was a very memorable thing to me. I felt that we were very much part of the local scene. There's two or three levels to what I'm calling the scene, but I think we were embraced. Certainly with a name like Creedence Clearwater Revival. I don't think we were really outsiders other than the fact that when it became known we made hit singles and pop music, and it became known that John Fogerty was kind of straighter than others when it came to chemicals.

But there were times when I have to say I looked at it with a bit of a jaundiced eye. We knew that many of those people came to San Francisco later. I also thought that the whole myth, the mythology of the San Francisco sound, was a concoction, almost like a Chamber of Commerce thing. Ralph J. Gleason did the liner notes to Creedence's first album. It covered the entire back of the LP, and happily in the very last sentence he mentioned our name. On our own record. The whole rest of the thing went "San Francisco is the center of the universe. Jefferson Airplane, Grateful Dead, Moby Grape, Quicksilver Messenger Service." And he ends, "in future years, everyone will know the San Francisco sound permeated the world, one of the greatest influences, whatever. Creedence Clearwater Revival is a fine example of the third generation of these musicians." What??? We had been there when those guys were off in Texas or someplace. So it kind of pissed us off. San Francisco sound, great. You mean, like Peter Wheat and the Breadmen? San Francisco sound. You mean like We Five? "Well I woke up this morning." It was sort of a concoction, and as our stature grew, as we got to play more and more places, we did meet some really nice people. Like Santana. Carlos was a smoking guitar player right from the get go and the band was hot and they were doing something quite different from everyone else. They were really relaxed and genuine. They were really nice people. Carlos and the guys in the band were up-and-coming at the same time. I was meeting guys with a dream in their eyes and going someplace. Whereas the Grateful Dead were always just sort of a little off from our circle. They did things differently. I never inhaled. I was really Mr. Straight. I was scared to death of LSD or any kind of pill. Yeah, I'd smoked some marijuana, and the other guys, I think, were certainly more experimental than me. But I didn't like it as an image. Since I was the leader, I was the guy with the whip saying, "Now, we're not going to push this as an image thing." But at the same time, I didn't feel that made us the Osmond Brothers either. And the Airplane, at least in those days, I always got this vibe from, an attitude, like Creedence somehow didn't fit into those circles. It was very real. I could never put my finger on what it was, but we were considered outsiders in our own town. (1997)

Doug Clifford

I enjoyed being a part of the scene, but I know what John's talking about. First of all, we didn't do drugs. We had a policy in the band. No drugs, no alcohol when we played, ever, and we adhered to that policy. Guys smoked pot and whatnot, but if anybody did it you did it at home and you didn't do it at work and that was it. Do what you want to at home, but make sure whatever it is you're doing doesn't affect what we do. That in itself made us kinda weird.

Second, playing kinda Southern rock and roll. We weren't playing psychedelic music. The first album had some hints of it, but that's as close as we got to it. From that standpoint, yeah, we weren't part of the scene. In fact, they used to call us the Boy Scouts of rock and roll. We never hung out with those guys, the Grateful Dead and people like that. We weren't part of the scene that way.

Interestingly enough, I ran into Spencer Dryden [of the Jefferson Airplane] at the twenty-fifth reunion of the Fillmore. That's when Bill Graham was alive, and Spencer was looking really rough. He said, "You know we used to make fun of you guys and call you a singles band but all of us would have died to have a hit single. We wanted hits so bad, and also the way you guys took care of yourselves and stayed away from drugs." He said, "Half of my friends are dead, and look at me, I'm burnt out." And he said, "I respect you for it," and I said, "Spencer, man, that took a lot of balls to say that," and I gave him a big hug.

That part of it was true, we were very straight. We'd worked a long time and we'd seen these other bands when they were all fucked up and high and they didn't sound very good. And we cared so much about the music and we'd worked so hard and we dared to be different. We dared to stick to the music that we loved and we didn't fall into a fad. We learned that with the Golliwogs, when we wore those suits. When we changed our way to Creedence Clearwater Revival, we said no more fads, no more silly stuff, none of that anymore, this is what we're gonna do. In terms of that I agree with John. Beyond that it was really a lot of fun just going to the Fillmore. It was a really neat scene going on. (1998)

Stu Cook

I loved it. I was deeply immersed in it. A lot of guys from other bands were friends of mine. I went to the ballrooms all the time. I didn't feel like

On the way up, 1970 *(Courtesy Graham Niven)*

an outsider. I was born in the Bay Area, this was happening in the Bay Area. San Francisco's a fantastic city, and it was the only place in the world where something like this could happen, so I just went to check it out and I found myself having a great time. I'm a young guy, single. This is great.

There was a lotta music. Some of it I liked better than others. There's no point trying to judge it, it just was. I went to see the Airplane and Moby Grape, Taj Mahal. We opened for Taj Mahal the only time we ever played the Avalon. I got into it. It was a great time. The whole thing was about hanging and being loose about stuff, it wasn't an uptight thing. I think John was more a part of it than he realized. You have interactions with people. Bill Graham liked us because we delivered. He had zero tolerance for artists who would shuck the audience.

One night we played the Fillmore West, the old Carousel Ballroom—the original Fillmore had closed and they were doing shows between Winterland and the Carousel on Market Street. It was almost at the peak of CCR's career and we were in our hometown. People just wouldn't let us go. We played everything we knew and rehearsed and then we started the show over again with "Born on the Bayou." We played seventeen encores. I think we played the whole show damn near twice, and we finally said, we gotta play again tomorrow night. That was a Saturday night.

So we came back Sunday, and somehow Bill Graham had gotten a jeweler to open up. And he bought us all Omega Seamaster gold watches and had engraved on the back: "To John, To Stu, To Tom, To Doug, with thanks, Bill Graham." And he gave us these watches, and he said, "You guys better retire now, 'cause this will never happen again."

We never really had a bad show. We had average shows and we had great shows and everything in between. But we knew our stuff well enough, it's not rocket science after all. It's all about entertaining, playing for people, giving them something. If you're honestly doing that, you'll get it back. That's what makes a great show. It doesn't matter what you're doing as long as you're committed and into it. (1998)

Most participants in the San Francisco scene attributed the group's position more to friendly rivalry than to any real animosity. Merl Saunders had known the group since its Golliwog days, while Rachel Donahue, the wife of pioneering underground radio DJ Tom Donahue, met them when she was working as KMPX's business manager.

Merl Saunders

It was like John said. They were outsiders. It was just a thing where it was a clique. They didn't hang around the Haight-Ashbury, they didn't get high, they didn't do drugs. They looked like little college students. You check those pictures out. They had striped coats with collars that buttoned, loafers, and stuff. Did Jerry [Garcia] look like that? (1998)

Rachel Donahue

They were in the East Bay and we used to tease him a little bit. It was two different kinds of music. It was the Grateful Dead and the Jefferson Airplane and Quicksilver Messenger Service who are long-haired hippie psychedelic and here was this guy across the East Bay doing this sort of Bayou rock and roll. I don't think he was an outsider at all, I think everybody accepted them. But John was always a little outside. Let's not forget the time he came back to the Fillmore dressed in a turquoise Elvis outfit. When they made *The Last Days of the Fillmore*. Everyone else was still looking like a hippie and he was wearing this turquoise, collar-up kind of suit. He'd been away a while. They were always major players. The most significant thing is they just seemed straight compared to the others. They were so much more disciplined in their music. They were much straighter, especially John, in his appearance. They were much more direct and to the point. There was no psychedelic babble involved in any of these things. They were pure rock and roll, they were commercial rock and roll, and I think that separated them from the rest of the groups that were considered to be part of the San Francisco scene.

People didn't dislike them at all. All the years I was at KSAN and KMPX they were played constantly, it was everyone's favorite music. If they felt they were outside other musicians, it was just a difference in attitude. Everybody loved Tom. John's not unlike Phil Spector in that he's a musical genius. His problem is, these are the guys there's never any room in the car for: "Hey, we'd love to take you, but there's not any room in the car." But I think that's what made his creative genius. He's not the warmest of people. I think he's wonderful, but this was peace, love, and happiness time and John isn't exactly a warm and fuzzy guy. I remember working on the Rick Dees show, and someone asked if he wanted to come back and do some liners in the back room, and he gave him such a withering look. I, however, took the traditional route and I baked him an apple pie. I remembered that was his favorite. (1998)

John Fogerty

In our case, I didn't think of it as the East Bay; I thought of myself as being in the tradition of rock and roll. This kind of mainstream rock line that comes down from 1953 or '54. I wanted to be in a Memphis rhythm section à la Elvis or Howlin' Wolf, you know. The San Francisco thing was just sort of its own quirky little deal. Intellectually or politically, I certainly felt akin to all that. We were all the same age, and all the same stuff was happening to us. But the music was too special. I really didn't like most of the drawn-out twenty-five-minute "ride-Trans-Love-Airlines" stuff the San Francisco groups were doing. My attention span wore out after ten minutes. (1985)

Tom Fogerty

John Phillips wrote the best song about the flower thing in San Francisco. The real good part of it, when the love thing just started. Phillips didn't live in San Francisco, but he wrote a song about it and captured it. Beautiful. He just felt something from it without really being there. (1970)

John Fogerty

We'd much rather play Fillmore West or Winterland than any place in the world, really. The shame of it is that now popularity sort of demands that we play a bigger place. So by doing benefits, we can still sneak back in and play where we really want to play, you know. Because good business, or whatever you want to call it, kind of dictates that you don't do that. If we were gonna have everyone see us who'd wanna see us, we'd have to play a week or something. Which we wouldn't want to do either. Four days used to be a real . . . you know, like four days at Winterland, it was a long time, you know! It starts to be like a club again. But the audiences are, I don't know what it is. Do they listen better? Or are they just more sophisticated? They laugh in the right places, like at a good movie. It's not ten seconds late, like some of the other stuff. They know what we're saying. They listen to the songs. . . . But anyway, this's our favorite place to play, especially, I'd say, really, the old Fillmore, which we only played once. It's such a treat. That was the first time we really heard ourselves with a good PA and everything. It spoiled us for anywhere else. As soon as we came into San Francisco-type places, we almost went immediately to the Fillmore. We sort of were able to get the gravy of San Francisco right away. It was a big change from NCO [noncommissioned officers] clubs and things, obviously. (1970)

Stu Cook

In 1964 the Free Speech Movement really changed Berkeley. We got student activism. Now—well, it's much more bohemian than it used to be. Berkeley before was really quiet. Like living in El Cerrito was so suburban—wow, I'm so goddamn middle class. But when there's not some big "cause," in quotes, the vibrations are really good in Berkeley. I don't know. Since you're asking me, I don't like to talk about it, but I think more in human values. Not slogans. Berkeley's Telegraph District is as hard as Haight for drugs. Outside of uptighting *[sic]* about speed and heroin, Berkeley is a friendly place, I guess. I mean there's a lot of hitchhiking and smiles on the streets. (1971)

Rachel Donahue

They brought their tapes up when they were the Golliwogs. If you brought a tape up we would play it, and [John] and Tom used to hang around a little bit while he was making the rest of the band rehearse in the garage. We were called underground. Tom [Donahue] always said it was like simultaneous discovery, like when everyone brings yo-yos to school at the same time. It was on everyone's mind, we just happened to be the first ones to pull it off full-time. He said everybody else could be first, he'd happily be second.

As soon as the station started making money, [owner] Leon Crosby decided we all had to wear suits and ties and straighten up, and he had been failing to meet the payroll a number of times, and we had to turn to alternative sources. Had a dope dealer dig up a coffee can and make everybody's payroll. So at one point he leaned out the window, yelling, please don't everybody go to the bank at once. They weren't going to pay us anything, but we had created something and now he wanted to change it. He wanted to bring in straight people, he wanted us to lose the beads, lose the hair, and nobody was having any part of it, so we made ridiculous demands, calling ourselves the AAIFMWW, the Amalgamated American

International FM Workers of the World. We hired a labor attorney who was in his eighties—he'd worked for the Mine Workers—and he guided us through a proper strike. We had benefits, people would bring down roach clips that had peace symbols on the top, and Bill Graham brought down a truck full of hams and all kinds of food, and we had fires in trash cans, and the first night Steve Winwood came down on a flatbed truck and played for the strikers. (1998)

John Fogerty

All the KMPX DJs walked out and said "at twelve o'clock we're all leaving"—that famous strike. Tom Donahue was the leader of the whole gang. We heard about it, we were playing at Deno and Carlo's, and we rushed right over to the station and set up all our equipment. We were the first band, in fact, we were the only band until the next morning about nine o'clock, more famous people got there like the Grateful Dead. But actually, Creedence Clearwater played there at one in the morning and people talked about the noise. It was the famous underground radio strike of 1968. (1998)

Rachel Donahue

We all walked out and we were out for a couple of months. We demanded double time on Halloween, we wanted the right to wear beads and bells and bangles and the right to burn incense in the studio. It was bordering on the ridiculous, and it was clear this little weasel was never going to take us back. He hated us even though we were making him money.

John signed the petition saying he wanted to withdraw his records, he didn't want his records played, and he'd support the strike, and it was a pretty big deal. It was the first time hippies had really made their presence felt, to know we actually had power, we had power to hurt people. We hurt that station pretty good. They never made it. (1998)

At the same time CCR was moving deeper into the San Francisco scene, its "Southern" sound was assuming its classic form. John Fogerty attributed the distinctiveness to his long-standing interest in black music.

John Fogerty

Our sound was a bit different [from the San Francisco sound] because I grew up in the East Bay and rock-and-roll radio and R & B radio were my teachers. The few shows I went to were usually at the Oakland Auditorium and the large majority were black entertainers doing rhythm and blues. This is the late fifties and early sixties, people like James Brown and the Midnighters and B. B. King and Ray Charles, Jackie Wilson, people who were rhythm and blues or else they were considered funky. I saw Duane Eddy there, believe it or not. I saw a show there that still sticks out in Duane's mind because he played there with B. B. King. B. B. King and I both for years have been telling Duane we sure liked that "Three Thirty Blues" he played there. I also went to a lot of folk music things, especially the old folk boom thing, 1959 or so. But I never considered that a pop music form, I considered that more my educational form, and what is really strange is that all these years later, people like Jorma [Kaukonen], from the Airplane, or Jerry Garcia, they were quite taken with that folk music boom. They're a couple of years older than me and they went off in that direction. Especially in Jorma's case. Jorma was a quite good finger-style guitar player. He kind of slaved under the masters, people like Reverend Gary Davis. He can play that stuff, so that influence went into his band big time. Whereas I favored the chicken-picking stuff like James Burton or Steve Cropper and I wasn't able to fingerpick very well, so the band that developed around me became more of a rhythm-and-blues Top Forty mode. I'm saying this with hindsight, but I think there's some substance to it. (1985, 1998)

Stu Cook

You gotta be associated with something. I think people have a hard time figuring out who you are. [The swamp rock label] helped. It wasn't intentional on our part, it was a media-generated thing. John's angle was to redo in a new way all the music we grew up with, especially blues and country and rock and some of the British influence as well. "Hey Tonight," for example, was a more modern reading of styles that had influenced us. It was a great experience. If people had known more about us, it would have been less interesting. Honestly, it worked well for us, it still works well. It's a term people still use to talk about new acts that have that kind of flavor. The sound of John's voice and the way we played together made it seem like we could have been Louisiana boys. Even people from Louisiana thought we were from Louisiana. (1998)

John Fogerty

I tried to make as many of the best type of rock-and-roll records as we could make. For me, a great rock-and-roll record must include these elements: First, foremost, it has a great title. Number two, it has a great sound. Number three, it should have a great song. In other words, something that really is valid and makes sense and, hopefully, you could sing without hearing the record. And number four, the best type of rock-and-roll record has a great guitar lick in it. I tried like crazy to come up with great guitar hooks to fashion a record around. I'm thinking of the kind of thing that began the song and defined the record. "Born on the Bayou," "Up Around the Bend," "Bad Moon Rising," even though it's just chords, there was a thing to it. "Centerfield." That hook, that guitar thing, is great. Another is "Green River." I think that's why the stuff is so popular. It's easy to listen to, it's simple to play, it sounds real good in a simple setting. You don't need a lot of equipment. It becomes magical even if you're in a bar in Winnemucca, which, believe me, I have heard. (1993)

I always thought that people who love rock and roll aren't necessarily *stupid*. If you can write a really good song and add good lyrics as icing, then it's even better, as long as you don't sacrifice the ethic of rock and roll in the first place. I like lots of stuff and I think I have a brain, and I consider my audience to be the same way. Instead of playing down to them, you're playing up to them. (1997)

I had a dream about ten years ago. The neatest dream since I was four, when I dreamed about Flash Gordon. This was a musical dream, like a song the Beatles do that changes speed and they just scream away. Anyway, there were a hundred acoustic guitars in this dream all hitting an E chord. Just hitting that chord. Everybody was together, just hitting those six hundred strings, making them sing. Man, I woke up and I've been trying to write a song for it ever since. Someday I'll do it, maybe use fifty overdubs to get that ringing sound. Two guitars together make an incredible ring. Especially if one is tuned to the chord. The Everly Brothers did that. That really psyched me out. Just all those guitars ringing. I only knew that one chord at the time. (1970)

Although in later years, Fogerty sometimes questioned his bandmates' musical ability, he always understood the central place of the rhythm section in Creedence Clearwater Revival's sound.

John Fogerty

The bass and drums are essentially the bottom for any rock band. That's the constant, solid thing—the foundation—and you build around it. When I'm writing music, I think bass and drums first. Like when I'm driving my car, I'll be singing doom, doom, doom or bappa bappa bop. That starts the songs. Everything else comes later. As I write the words, I'm also writing the melody and the bass line and drum part. It all happens at once. I don't actually write it, it all happens in my head. As we go along I'll be specific less and less. We're all learning what we have to learn. I want to hear them get it the most comfortable way first before I decide whether or not to dump it. I make sure I hear it the way I felt it in my head before I decide it's good or bad. I want them to come up with ideas, too, because I wouldn't be taking advantage of their knowledge. (1970)

Stu Cook

As we played together, we got better together. We developed an additional sense, an innate feel for where each other was going. You speed up a little here, then you pull back a little bit here. We got to where we just knew when that was comin'. A bass player and a drummer really have to be tight, so I just work off his foot. If he picks it up a little bit, if we go into a chorus and the energy builds a little bit. Even guys who program synthesizers, when they go into a chorus, kick it up a beat or two a minute to give it a live thing. Into the chorus everybody's supposed to hit it. We weren't examples of any kind of technical virtuosity in those days, but we got the job done. We weren't any better or worse than anybody else we were playing with. (1998)

73

Doug Clifford

Stu's just great, he's solid. We're like a hand in a glove. We know what we're thinkin' without thinkin'. It's like riding a bike. I have a certain style on drums, it's a feel style, I'm not fancy. It's simple but it's distinctive. You can hear a track and say, "That's Clifford playing drums." There's a book Joe Smith wrote, and John says, "It took me a long time to able to say this, but we were a darn good band, and at our peak, no one could top us. There might have been other musicians on paper who were better man for man, but no one could top us. We were guys who didn't have any help. It shows you what four guys can do when they work together."

That's what it's about. We were always dedicated to that guy. All of us were dedicated to the band. We did our very best, and I'm proud of my work. And now, it's so sad. The guy just doesn't get it, and, unfortunately, I don't think he can fully enjoy the fruits of his labor. It was a wonderful thing. It was a dream of schoolboys growing up, the American dream. That in itself is wonderful, it doesn't get any better than that.

In 1968, "Suzie Q" provided CCR with its long-awaited breakthrough, eventually reaching number eleven on the national charts. The follow-up, "I Put a Spell on You," reached number fifty-eight.

Stu Cook

We were playing five nights a week, five sets a night, up at this little dump in Sacramento out near one of the air force bases. We have, like, four bucks in the bank, five bucks in the bank, it was single-digit bank account time. We miraculously got this union-scale gig playing up there.

We didn't have enough material to play that much, so we had to play

P.O. BOX 9246   •   BERKELEY, CALIFORNIA 94709

Dear Creedence Fan:

Thank you for becoming a member of the Creedence Clearwater
Revival Fan Club, the official one. We're glad you decided
to share a bit of your life with us and hope your thoughts
will be just a little groovier than they might have been
before you opened this envelope.

We want to thank you, too, for the support you've given us
through the years. We'll not soon forget the folks who came
to see us play, even when we were nobody. Nor could we dis-
regard all the fine letters people have taken the time to
write. (We still have every one of them.)

Our fan club is geared to honesty and a smile. If you were
expecting "full-color super-pix" (!) of John with his shirt
off, (Ohhhhh! Dreammmmy!) you may be disappointed with this
whole affair. Sorry. If, however, you are genuinely interested in what we are doing, who we really are, and what our
lives are all about; then, welcome to the club!

John Fogerty   Tom Fogerty

Doug Clifford   Stu Cook

A welcome to the CCR fan club *(Courtesy Graham Niven)*

'em over, take special requests. We hadn't been playing "Suzie Q" for years. We used to play it all the time, when we heard the Dale Hawkins single. When the Stones did it we were already playing "Last Time," "Satisfaction," all the big Stones tunes, so we just dropped "Suzie Q" because we liked our version better and we didn't want to have to learn it like the Stones, so we just left it. So we're playing this toilet up there, so I said to John, "Why don't we take 'Suzie Q,' we haven't done it for years, let's turn it into a psychedelic jam. We'll play the song, we'll do a solo that follows the verse chord changes, then we'll come back and do another verse and you can just play for ten minutes."

And that's the arrangement we recorded. I suggested that we come back to that kind of approach to it just for expediency, just to get through the night. It was a perfect way to change a set, and people were digging that long stretched-out thing, so it came back in fine form. Then Bill Drake's radio syndication organization heard it and put it on all their stations, and that was the beginning right there. Radio's always been a strong supporter of Creedence. They've helped us way more than our record company has. (1998)

Merl Saunders

I was on the road when I heard this record called "Suzie Q." I turned it up and I said, that sounds like John. I heard it every half hour, and I said, that *is* John, but I don't know who this Creedence Clearwater is. I *think* that's John singing. It kinda blew me away. (1998)

John Fogerty

Before that, everything kind of sounded like "Fight Fire" or "Brown-Eyed Girl" or something. When we would play out, we were more rock and roll. We had a few R & B tunes that we did. We did "In the Midnight Hour," like every band in the world. I knew we were into something kind of original, kind of new. We rehearsed "Suzie Q" every day for months. We just played that song over and over. We played a ten-, twelve-minute version every time, just to try and get that feel of the groove and come up with that cohesiveness that was really above us at the time.

I told Saul Zaentz about wantin' to do "Suzie Q," wantin' to do "Spell." In fact, he'd come over and seen us at Deno and Carlo's and he said, "Well, I think you guys should make an album." Which we'd talked about loosely for four years, but never gotten around to it, you know. But we went in and did "Suzie Q"—the whole idea behind doing somebody else's tune was, then I could worry about the sound, and, you know, the musicianship on the record. I wouldn't be so involved with my own tune and I'd be all hung up on phrasing, and all this kind of stuff, and the meaning of the words. It was a tune that I had liked for ten, twelve years. We'd been playing it for seven or eight years. So I didn't have to worry about that. All I had to worry about was the producing end, you know. He agreed that that was a good idea, so we did "Suzie Q" as really a demonstration tune. Hopefully we could get it on the radio. And so that was like our combination of everything we knew. And we did it on "Suzie Q." We went in, and we were so ready to do it, it was one take all the way through! Just whap! And that was that. It's the same exact version as on the LP, nothing changed at all. I did the whole thing with it in mind of being a single eventually. That's why all the interesting stuff happens at the beginning. All the vocals are at the beginning. I visualized it as two parts so we could cut it in half later. I saw nothing wrong, artistically, with that. (1970)

This little underground San Francisco radio station, KMPX, would play all kinds of weird things. It's been said that what we were doing seemed very far removed from the rest of San Francisco, but that's not quite true. "Suzie Q" was designed to fit right in. The eight-minute opus. Feedback. Like the Butterfield Blues Band's "East-West." And especially the little effect, the little telephone box in the middle, which is the only part I regret now. It's just funny-sounding. But, lo and behold, it worked. (1993)

What happened was, KMPX had the tapes, and then there was the strike. Then, our album was completed the same week KSAN came on, with the new guys [DJs]. So we took a tape of the new album over there. And I think it was from then on that I knew everything was going to be all right. From the very first day. We had supported the strike pretty strongly, but they didn't really owe us anything. In other words, what happened following us taking the tape wasn't a payoff or anything.

We walked in with the tape unleadered or anything. [The tracks] just ran right together for however long the album is. And they said, "What's a good cut to play?" And I said, "Well, the first one, I guess. Start right at the beginning with 'Spell.'" And they played that, then they just played it right through for like a week and a half. It was incredible! You know, the airplay. And the album wasn't even released yet. It was still a tape. The album came out and, for a relatively unknown group, sold. It was incredible how it sold! And I knew right then that everything was all right.

"Suzie Q" wasn't released as a single till August. Which was two and a half or three months later. Actually, "I Put a Spell on You" and "Suzie Q" were released together as two singles. We were playing at the Cheetah, in L.A. It was a real drag. We drove down in the Volkswagen bus. Saul'd talked us into it, because it was good for exposure. Sometimes that makes it, but we didn't want to pay any more dues, really. Little did we know what the next year was going to be! Whew! But we thought, "Gee, for ten years, we've done all that junk, and now we've got almost a hit record," you know. We could see the importance was in the records. They could do the work for us, if we let 'em, if we were patient. But Saul really wanted us to go down there, because some record people would come, and we said, "Okay." And we went. And he showed up down there, which was far out, he and an L.A. distributor. . . . And he told us that [Top Forty programmer] Bill Drake had just put it on, I think, the Chicago station and one other station. . . . Mainly he told us that Drake liked "Suzie Q." Which to us was really far out! We were convinced it would never happen. Underground sensations, and that was that. He told us Bill Drake liked the record and it was almost a cinch from there. There was still that ulcer . . . waiting and waiting and waiting for something to happen. I think *then* was the first real indication. (1970)

We stepped into the next dimension with "Suzie Q." I kind of did the same thing around that same time with the song "I Put a Spell on You." It helped define us. It was obviously another place from where we had been for ten years. In other words, it was all right for John, the white kid from El Cerrito, to sing this stuff, even though it had that attitude. I wasn't directly mimicking a blues player or an R & B player. Because so many of those experiments don't work. They just don't work. In fact, there's things on Creedence's first album where we're kind of dangerously close to trying to be blues and it didn't work. But "Suzie Q" and "I Put a Spell on You" were both sort of new blendings of the worlds between pop, rock and roll, R & B, and a slight amount of country in there. (1997)

There are a lot of other things on the album. I got the inspiration for "The Working Man" from all the jobs we've ever had outside of the band. Two of us worked in a gas station, which is probably the closest identity to that song. Doug was a janitor, and we've also driven trucks. There's some humor in the song, but it's also sad. You spend all your paycheck on the weekend and start over again making it on Monday. "Get Down Woman" is just my tribute to that old swing-shuffle thing. The words are secondary to the music. I just got that one little guitar riff and built the whole song around it. I don't particularly like swing jazz, but I love it in a blues. I also love good brass and walking bass in that rhythm. But we don't perform many songs like that because people don't dance to that rhythm anymore. It used to make the rhythm-and-blues charts. It's not loud and exciting enough for today. (1969)

CCR continued to polish its live act. The venues were better than those of a few years before. In May 1968, they played the Avalon Ballroom on a bill with Taj Mahal. In July, they played the Fillmore West with the Paul Butterfield Blues Band. In July 1969, they again played the Fillmore, this time on a bill with Fleetwood Mac. When the band traveled, it no longer played roadhouses, but major clubs such as the Cheetah in Los Angeles, where it shared a bill with Howlin' Wolf. The foundation for the success, however, had been laid down at Bay Area clubs such as Deno and Carlo's.

Stu Cook

It took a time to build an audience, until we found a couple of clubs that we could play in. One club in particular called Deno and Carlo's. I never did meet Carlo, but Deno was there all the time. We got to play there one night every week. We chose an off night so it didn't conflict with any real paying gigs. All our fans would come on that night. Another night was another band's, and their fans would be there. So we were always playing to people who wanted to hear us, and we developed. Some of the music for the first album was fine-tuned there, but most of *Bayou Country* was developed in that club, played for those people before we ever went into the studio with it. (1997)

John Fogerty

When we played Deno and Carlo's we were calling ourselves Creedence Clearwater Revival. We had that engagement in 1968, beginning in

March or April. The tape of "Suzie Q"—it wasn't a record yet—the tape was being played on KMPX. They were playing it a lot because it was groovy psychedelic music. Each week I'd send Ralph Gleason, who had a column in the *San Francisco Chronicle*, a card with simply the information that we were playing at Deno and Carlo's on Monday night. Basically, I turned that into Creedence night. So dutifully, every Sunday or every Monday morning in his column he would report among other tidbits of local news that Monday night Creedence Clearwater is playing at Deno and Carlo's. As long as I kept sending the letter, he would report it. I was afraid if I didn't send him the letter he might miss, so I sent it to him every single week. That was great. That was free publicity. The record company sure wasn't doing anything. That was John Fogerty's approach to management and publicity. I was the PR guy. And it was kinda working. The crowd would get steadily larger each week. I suppose we were there for three or four months. One time I came to the crowd and announced that LBJ had just been on TV and said he's not running for president. PR guy and newsman. (1998)

We played the Cheetah, for which we never got paid. . . . And we went down and we found out Howlin' Wolf was on the bill, and we were top billing, which was great. We felt good and all that, but it was also a drag. Because Howlin' Wolf was there, and he got, I think, last billing. We got lots of time, you know, when you're young, and we knew we were gonna make it. It was like a drag, because he's at the end of his thing. And it was really kind of upsetting. It's like you wish they could give him a gold record, I don't know. I'm superromantic about it, I guess. It's like Jackie Robinson in baseball. It's the same thing. These are the guys that started it, that made it. There were so many, they were so good, they couldn't ignore 'em anymore, but what they finally started doing was, they had the white imitations on. The thing with the Crewcuts, with the Diamonds. Or Georgia Gibbs doing a LaVern Baker record. (1969)

Stu Cook

Did you hear what Chess did to Wolf? They shoved him into a Cream thing. Of course, Cream never said they were a blues band, but they incorporated that into Wolf's thing. I saw a photo of Wolf at the session. He's sitting there with his head in his hands like he's saying, "What in hell am I doing?" It's terrible. We played a show with him in Los Angeles and, man, it was a real treat. He just played the old blues. Too much. Some guys wanted to jam with him after. They got there and turned up their amps and tried to get into some slide-guitar stuff. Wolf packed up and went home. He was there to play music. (1970)

CCR's real arrival came with the release of "Proud Mary" in March 1969. From the first notes, the song established the swamp rock sound that received its classic expression on the Bayou Country *album. Although CCR never had a number one single, "Proud Mary" was the first of five that reached number two. (The others were "Bad Moon Rising," "Green River," "Travelin' Band," and "Lookin' Out My Back Door.")* Bayou Country *reached the top ten on the album charts and was the group's first million-selling LP.*

John Fogerty

I carried "Proud Mary" around as an arrangement for a long time as a concept for a record, the sound I carried around for quite a while. But I didn't have a title and I didn't have a melody. And I finally got my discharge from the army, so two days later I wrote "Proud Mary." It was very personal to me. Even though I didn't put it in a setting of the army, or that sort of thing—you know, who cares—my real dream, I think, all of my life, was to do what the guy in "Proud Mary" does. It's an escape, so it finally comes out that way—but I kept writing words right up to the last day before we recorded it. I knew as soon as the basic tracks for the record were done that that would be our big one.

In the middle of July 1968, this envelope containing this little thing that's like a diploma had been sitting on the stairs of my apartment building for a couple of days. It said, "Official Business," or something. Well, I didn't bother to look close at it. Finally, one day I was coming into my apartment, and I look on the stairs, and, "Hey, that's got my name on it!" Well, son of a bitch, I opened it up, and I'm discharged from the army. Holy hallelujah! I actually went out on the little apartment building lawn and did a couple of cartwheels. At that one moment it was like, "Wow, all the troubles of the world have been lifted off my shoulders!"

If it didn't happen within five minutes, certainly within a week and a half I had written "Proud Mary." That one event that led to doing the cartwheels, that's where "Left a good job in the city" comes from. I just felt real good. Although I didn't recall it at the time when I was doing "Rollin' on the river," there is an old Will Rogers movie about these old paddle wheelers, and I believe at one point they actually sing, "Rolling on the river." I know that buried deep inside me are all these little bits and pieces of Americana. It's deep in my heart, deep in my soul. As I learned in English 101, write about what you know. (1993)

The solo in "Proud Mary" was sort of me doing Steve Cropper. And when I found the right one, I didn't see any reason to change it. There's a certain kind of "bing"—you hit the right note or chord and that's it. The universe goes, "harmony," and everything fits into place. I see no reason to change that if it seems so right. (1985)

We don't play Bayou anything. Our music is not Bayou music, in sound or musical harmony or anything. What we do is, we marry the sound of our music, what it's doing, with what the song is about—very well I think. Like "Proud Mary," the first chords to me, that really sounded like a paddle wheel going around. But it's not based on any real geographical influence as far as the music's concerned. I guess the only thing that's weird about it is that I was from *here* and not from *there*. That's really the only unique part. I guess, mainly most of the people I saw that I really liked came from there or *seemed* to come from there. Fats Domino. I always pictured Jerry Lee Lewis as being from there. For sure, Elvis *must* have been from there. Carl Perkins, and the whole Sun Records thing . . . I guess that's all been said. It really becomes a kind of cliché. To me, it's very personal. But I find myself saying the same thing again. I'm not trying to break my arm patting myself, but the idea was, well, there's so much bad rock and roll and all we did was to sort of clean it up and make it, not more traditional, just not so darned irritating. You know, cleaner or something. Take "Born on the Bayou." The music was supposed to be just sort of a funky rock and roll, sort of a Bo Diddley—people told me that later— sort of slow and soulful kinda music. But it had nothing to do with anything I'd ever heard on the Bayou or anything. The song, yes, that was like that kind of fantasyland I had developed over the years. But the sound of the music, no. And therefore you shouldn't say "Bayou rock" or any of that sort of thing. (1970)

I would sit there, kind of look at the blank wall in my little apartment, and I just kind of pictured this story. Now around this same time, because of "Suzie Q" getting played on the underground radio station, we played the Avalon Ballroom, in San Francisco. We were on stage for a two-minute sound check. I started doing this thing with the guitar, and I started screaming into the microphone what would later become a refined melody but at that moment was just noise, and I had Doug and Stu just play along. I just wanted to hear this energy thing. Anyway, that mythical thing that I was dreaming up at night and that burst of energy on the stage at the Avalon came together. "Born on the Bayou" is almost the Gordian knot or the key to what happened later. As I was writing it, it occurred to me that there was more power than just this one song. If there was a way

84

to tie it all together on one album, kind of cross-fertilize, cross-relate the songs, you would have a much more interesting and maybe more powerful image. So that's what happened. "Born on the Bayou" sort of relates to "Proud Mary." It certainly relates to "Keep on Chooglin'" and "Graveyard Train." (1993)

Doug Clifford

My favorite record of ours is "Born on the Bayou." It's just an ass-kicker and a rolling track and, basically, where that song started was at the Shrine Auditorium in Los Angeles. The boys got all their new toys. The Kustom amps were supposed to show up that night and, by God, they did. They're out there playing with them and getting sounds, and here I am with the same set. John's out there working with feedback, sorting that out, and I was tapping here and there and they're telling me, "Be quiet," and I got tired of it and I just started out with that quarter-note beat that I played on "Suzie Q" but I changed the foot pattern, and that was sort of the beginning on it. That's how it started, that feedback beginning and that quarter-note beat. (1998)

Stu Cook

Bayou Country really set the tone for what the band was about. That album was played live. Those songs were tried out on the audience at Deno and Carlo's. We all had a feel for the music together. That was pretty much the last album that had any seasoning before we took it to tape. I like the sound on that album. It's the fattest sound of any of the Creedence albums, bigger bass, richer, warmer. I think it fit the swamp handle better.

The other stuff got to be a little thin in the bottom. We went to a different studio, different engineer. We picked up Russ Gary with *Green River*. The mix was a problem from the beginning. It's not a question of, should my instrument be louder, it's more a question of where it's fitting in the mix. If it's the bass it should be rich and warm and fill that bottom. One could say it's not loud enough, but the real point is, it doesn't sound right in the blend. It doesn't have to drown something else out. There's nothing else going on in the lower frequency but the bass and the bass drum. The bass drum has a lot of attack on it, a lot of midrange frequency so you can hear it popping. So really you've got the bass guitar down there that has to fill that spectrum, and it doesn't have to drown out the bass drum to do that. Or anything else. It doesn't have to drown out the guitar or the tambourine.

A well-mixed record should take this stuff into consideration. You deal with that in the mix if you haven't recorded it exactly right. We [Stu and Doug] were excluded from the mixing of the records because we had suggestions or comments that for one reason or another couldn't or wouldn't be dealt with. In several articles, John's said, "I never let 'em in again." Well, for my money the albums suffered. I think they could have sounded better. I would have liked to have felt a little more of my instrument. We got back to a little better sound on *Pendulum*, but that was too far the other way. I would have liked to have gone farther toward "Good Golly Miss Molly" and "Proud Mary." (1998)

"Proud Mary" and Bayou Country *catapulted CCR into the middle of a scene much larger than the one in the Bay Area. Interviewers frequently asked Fogerty to comment on the "competition."*

John Fogerty

I'd have to say the Beatles are my favorites. Whatever they do is right.

They're the best at whatever they do, always number one. I like what the Beatles do with their voices. To me, I picture them more as kind of everyday musicians who sing, rather than as singers, you know? Every once in a while Paul, especially, will knock me out. It's so classy. It's above just the regular rock and roll kind of thing. They're talented in a lot of areas, which is the difference. They can do the songwriting and all that, but they can get the production jobs, too, and twenty-five percent in each of those'd be enough, and they do it, like, one hundred percent. They're really good in each one of 'em. Everything has been said about *Sgt. Pepper*, but it has to be the all-time greatest album. It's a total album rather than twelve tunes tied together. Anything the Beatles ever did has been done well, but *Sgt. Pepper* is a milestone. For the Beatles' career, it was a culmination and a departure at the same time. It changed them and solidified them. It was much more than just a record.

I like Stevie Winwood, Van Morrison, and Richie Havens as vocalists. Traffic is my next favorite group. In blues, it's always been B. B. King. There's never been anyone as good as him and there might never be. Modern blues is more pop, like Wilson Pickett and the Atlantic/Stax thing. I'd say our whole group agrees to Booker T. and the MGs as the best band. No matter what they do we dig it, especially their old work with Otis Redding and Sam and Dave. They're the best rock-and-roll band of all time, bar none. They each have different personalities, and when they're the MGs they have one personality and then when they back other Stax artists they have another. Al Jackson is my primo choice for what a rock drummer ought to be. His feeling is greater than any drummer I've heard.

A lot of white people are getting heavily into Negro music, but still, nobody comes close to B. B. King. White people have to organize things better, which is part of our civilization. Beethoven is beautiful, probably the finest example of man's mind as applied to civilized Western music.

You wouldn't say that about Muddy Waters, but therein lies the beauty of Muddy's blues. You have to use different measuring sticks to get into different kinds of music. (1968)

The release of "Bad Moon Rising" in June 1968 made it clear that "Proud Mary" was no fluke and solidified CCR as a commercial and creative force. But it was the B side, "Lodi," that established the group as an American myth. Every garage band in the United States could relate to Fogerty's images of trying to keep the faith in the music "while people sat there drunk." It wasn't an accident that Fogerty's blues hymn to a shared loneliness became a staple in the repertoires of bands playing the Lodi equivalents from Pennsylvania and Georgia to Colorado and Oregon.

In almost every interview from that time, Stu Cook, Doug Clifford, and Tom Fogerty presented the group as a representation of the sixties' highest communal ideals. Once it was in a financial position to do so, the group expanded its community by hiring old friends to handle equipment, publicity, and the hundreds of details that sometimes made it hard to concentrate on music.

Stu Cook

[Tour manager] Bruce Young used to hang around with us and help set up the equipment when we were at Deno and Carlo's. At the time he was working as a youth counselor in a juvenile detention center. [Equipment man Bruce Kourtz] was Tom and Doug's mailman, while Ray Francoise, who is our other equipment man, was originally our butcher. [Press officer] Jake Rohrer, like everyone else, is an old friend, from our high school days. At one time Jake was an auto salesman, and it just so happened that we all had French cars in various roadworthy conditions. When we were all broke, which was quite often the case then, Jake used to fit us all with spare parts, never asking for payment. As soon as

Creedence got enough bread together, we hired them all. And that's how we've remained. (1971)

John Fogerty

We have *excellent* people working for us. We have two equipment managers and one, like, road manager. My youngest brother, Bob, is our photographer-in-residence. He doesn't play a guitar but comes up with some splendid camera work. Our secretary, Mary Walsh, is much involved with fan matters and the fan club, does a good bit of PR work, some artwork, and occasionally brings in a goodie from her kitchen for everyone to freak out on. Lastly but by no means least is Jake Rohrer, the front man. Jake is the press officer, oversees the fan club and the fan club magazine, raps with people on the phone, and generally sees that things get done. And I've been grooming them for the past year, year and a half. Really cocky, but I know they'll know which way to move because they learned it from me. At least they'll agree with me, you know!

We want to handle our own booking. It'll be like a copartnership. We'll be the promoter. In other words, it'll be our money and that sort of thing. They'll oversee the details . . . advertising . . . they'll get the sound company we want, but they'll make sure they're doing it. And then, of course, they'll take care of the tickets and all that.

Doug Clifford

The group is my life and my personal challenge. The music for me is a highly personal form of communication and one that breaks down walls of language between people. If music helps people communicate, that's important. If it makes them feel good, too, as I think ours does, that's just as important. (1970)

Stu Cook

Creedence Clearwater Revival is definitely a fifth person. Outside of the four of us. I like to think of that fifth individual as a perfect blend of art and science and one that voices both. All the notes have been played before so there's nothing new scientifically. Artistically, I feel we're injecting something new and with good taste. The whole is bigger than any individual. Like a marriage, only there's four personalities instead of two. Each one of us will make allowances for the other. The road is fun because it's fun to get together—but we never all four lived together. That would be fatal. (1970)

Tom Fogerty

John and I have always been brothers, obviously. But we regard ourselves just as friends. That's the way it is with the group too. We've been together for ten years. We've got a unity of minds. Our goal has been constant . . . to make it in music, but only after making it together as people. (1970)

Even back then, John Fogerty's statements sounded a slightly different note. Where his bandmates talked of "we," Fogerty's contemporary descriptions of the group's process placed an unmistakable emphasis on his individual struggle to realize a creative vision. From time to time, rumors have surfaced that Fogerty played all of the instruments himself, sneaking back into the studio and rerecording parts after the group recording had been completed. Everyone, including Fogerty, has steadfastly denied these rumors. Still, there seems little doubt that once the group entered the studio, it was John who made the crucial decisions. He took special pride in his efficiency as a producer. According to a Fantasy spokesman, CCR's early albums cost about two thousand dollars each to produce, as compared to an industry average of around fifty thousand dollars.

John Fogerty

Probably ninety-nine percent of the tracks we did as a quartet are played live, with all four guys playing at the same time. I've heard the rumor over the years that "after they left the studio, John went in and rerecorded all the parts." No. I think the charm of what you hear on those records is four guys really playing. As far as learning studio techniques, prior to 1964 I spent about four thousand hours hanging around in little studios. I played on some sessions, but mainly I just watched and listened and learned. I was just freelancing in funky little studios. I played harp, guitar, piano, or just clapped my hands. I did it for free, just to learn. Mainly because most musicians are just treated like a piece of meat when a producer gets them.

Guys used to say, "It seems like John was born with an eight-track machine in his head." I actually started playing around with that when I was still in ninth grade. I bought this Sony tape recorder that had a tweed covering on it. It had built-in speakers and what they called "add-a-track." You could record something on the first track and then play that back and play along with it on the second track, so you were adding to it. I learned how to add three or four parts, and that I had to add the thing I wanted loudest last so that it was the cleanest. A lot of my arranging skill came from being able to experiment with that when I was fifteen or sixteen years old. (1970)

We made, I guess, five or six records before we ever went to Fantasy. We did a lot of instrumentals and that sort of thing. As a group, we recorded two thousand hours in the studio. And then I would go in and be a sideman or whatever with country and western or polkas. You know, whatever you want, we'd play it, just to learn what a studio was about. I knew it would come in handy some day. . . . So I began to see there was a sort of method to all this madness. . . . I mean you turn on one microphone and a certain thing happens. You put on a little echo and that happens. So that now from the very conception of a song I know what it's going to be like. There's no surprises, ninety percent anyway. Sometimes it just doesn't work out at all. It's terrible, you know. And *that's* a surprise!

We put the vocals on after we do the instrumental part. In other words, I sing live in the studio. But we only record the instrumental parts, because, if you have a vocal mike on, all that noise goes into the vocal mike, too. The vocals being obviously softer than the drums and the guitar. And it makes for a pretty crummy sound. Everything's kind of *sksksksheww!* So we record what we call a basic track first. We do that on four tracks, so that we don't have to spend a lot of time in the studio balancing stuff. If each guy's played his part right, I can balance it later.

In the old days, like with old Fantasy, we'd spend hours working on one take. We'd be playing it okay each time, but, "Oh, the bass's too loud. Turn it down." That kind of thing. . . . Every once in a while there's a little leakage, like with my voice through the guitar mike or through the drum mike if I don't sing it exactly the same, which I don't usually. There'll be a few phrases way off there in the background coming through.

The idea is, we use the term "basic track" to mean the four instruments we play all the time. We base everything on the basic track, really. Once we've got that, everything else is okay. But if the basic track's no good, there's no way you can clean it up. Sometimes I'll use the tape echo or the repeat, that kind of thing. But even for the drums and stuff, we try and make everything sound as natural as it is in person. What it is, we should get that sound first. Just when we sit down to practice we should be able to put a mike in front and record it, you know. We don't spend hours and hours, getting the sound this way and that. We do spend about one hour each time we record, getting the mixture right and that sort of thing. They've got shelves of that kind of thing in the studio, they can change everything. Maybe sometime, in the future, I'll use it for effect. Just to try out, like another instrument. But ninety percent of the time it's just straight through.

A studio doesn't inspire me one bit. So I can't sit down, like at a typewriter, in the studio, and wait for something to come. It wouldn't happen. In fact, it used to be totally impossible. Because I was worried about that clock! You know, spendin' all that money! Every hour that would go around really bugged me. Now, I really zip through. I really do. We'll go in, we'll have maybe ten tunes, unfinished, and I'll go in, and in four or five hours, we'll do all the little things and finish them. I like to work that way. I gotta have an engineer that really plays ball with me, really rolls along, because I've done all the thinking previously. I don't like to sit around and wait to be inspired in the studio. I want to get it done so we can go on to the next material. If it hangs around inside too long, it becomes stale. In the studio you're running against the clock, so you say, "Hey, that's great," but when you get home you figure it could have been better.

For the same reason we steer clear of fads like fuzz and wah-wah. It's been used well, a couple of times, but it's going to go out. We want our music to last a while, be part of a continuous thread. Stay on the main line rather than go off on side trips. (1970)

The tension between communal myth and individual process that can be glimpsed in the statements the group made at the time has become a dominant theme in the band members' retrospective comments on CCR. Cook attributes the origin of the problems to business issues, while Fogerty emphasizes creative concerns.

Stu Cook

When John went in to try to renegotiate the band's contract before *Green*

River, what he really did was, he went in to try to get his songs back. They said, no you can't have your songs back. So he said, how about the deal you promised us? They wanted to do something else. They didn't want to give us the money, they wanted to give us a piece of the company, which we didn't want. At the time we wanted the money. John couldn't get anywhere with them, and he just withdrew and he wouldn't even tell us for six weeks. Finally, Doug said, "What happened with our negotiations? You're in a deep funk here. You went in to get us a better record deal." He said, "Fantasy said no." Doug said, "Why don't we just stop giving them product? They're an independent company, they don't get paid for *Bayou Country* until they ship *Green River.* Why don't we grab 'em by the nuts?"

But John was so afraid we'd fall off the face of the earth at that point that we doubled our product input to them. We had three albums that year. We had a chance where we could have broke them. At that point we could have gotten a good entertainment attorney. Doug put it right out there for him. That was where we started going, "Hey, wait a minute. We want some input into our own lives." The roots of the later problems started way back at *Bayou Country.* (1998)

John Fogerty

Tom did not understand the role of the producer, so it was like every other band you've ever heard of. It was like a cartoon to me. When I mixed "Suzie Q" they were present in the studio. This was one of those studios where the mixing console was raised, and then from down in front of it, you could look out into the recording studio. . . . This was at Coast Recorders. . . . So there were some seats down in front of the console where hangers-on could look out into the studio, but they were not looking at the mixing console. So while I was doing "Suzie Q," the one

Heading up around the bend *(Courtesy Graham Niven)*

and only time they were there during a Creedence mix, I kept hearing, "That's not going to work!" and "Oh, that's too loud!" and "Aw, that'll never . . . " You know, that sort of thing for the whole two hours . . . I let it happen only one time, even though I was only twenty-two years old. When it was all mixed and mastered and they heard it, they said, "John, how did you know all that background vocal stuff was going to work?" And I said, "Because I mapped it out. I knew what I was going to do before I got in there." And they said, "Well, we didn't think . . . " And I said, "Yeah, I *know* you didn't think it was going to work. And that's the last time you're ever going to be around when I'm doing it." And that was it. I never let them be in there again. Every song after that, I just refused to let them be there, because it was so disruptive. It's like that with every single band in the world, especially when they're young. They have no concept of what a producer does—they just know they played this part, their little drum part, or their rhythm part or whatever. They go into the control room, and the rhythm guitar player hollers, "I can't hear my part," so of course the guy defers to him and turns up the rhythm guitar. Then the bass guy comes in and screams, "I can't hear *my* part," and he turns up the bass part. And then the background singer comes in, "I can't hear my part." Shit, you can't have everybody louder than everyone else; you're not making a record when you do that. It was a go-around I had with Tom for the whole three years we were Creedence. He kept saying, "My part's not loud enough."

I was always a team player. I had created this entity, and I was doing what a CEO today would call marketing. I was trying to present the image of a group and that we were all this band of happy lads, much like the Beatles. And so years later I was still trying to defer to their egos and not make it look any other way. But the truth is, I would write the song, and then the producer in me would take over and write the arrangement, and I would show everybody *exactly* how it went. If you're going to go in and record, everybody's got to have a specific part, otherwise you have a train wreck—it's just going to be noise.

So I arranged everything, quite specifically, much in the way Benny Goodman did with his swing band. There are only a couple of right ways to play a song, and there are a a whole lot of wrong ways. With most Creedence songs, the arrangements were based on a groove or a rhythm. I've had people tell me, "Gee, you've always had this great groove going on in the background." Well, that's not an accident, that's what I wanted. You have to figure out what it is that grooves. Only a few things are going to work. Let's say you've figured out the guitar; then you've got to figure out the bass part, and the rhythm guitar part, and the drums that complement that, because you still have a myriad of choices that could screw up your initial choice on the lead guitar. So it was very much chosen and arranged before they even heard the song. I would show the guys in the band what to play. And in some cases, it got really touchy, especially as we made our way along the successful path we were taking. Their egos got more and more sensitive, to where I actually had to spoon-feed them the parts. I remember when I was showing Stu "Down on the Corner," he was having a hell of a time with it. I was showing him one or two notes at a time, so that it evolved to where he thought he invented the part. I'd say, "Well, try going . . . " and he'd play those, and then I'd say, "Well, what if you did this next?" So by the time he got done, he actually thought he invented it, but I had worked it out a couple of weeks before. (1997)

Stu Cook

John thinks that he is Creedence. He describes Creedence alternately as this cartoon character or this ugly misshapen brother kept in the closet. He actually said he taught us how to play. We were as good as he was at the time. We grew together, we learned how to play together. John says, I want you to play this note and this note, but I knew how to play them. I actually practiced my instrument, learned all of Duck Dunn's bass parts with the MGs and Otis. I took it somewhat seriously myself. I never made my living any other way than being a musician. I've taken it seriously from the beginning.

To say that I thought I invented the part to "Down on the Corner," which I've seen floating around in various interviews. "Down on the Corner" is a guitar riff; I play note for note what John is playing on the guitar. So I can say that truly, I had virtually zero input into that bass line, I'm playing the guitar part. It didn't take me two weeks to learn it and I didn't think that I had invented it by the time the two weeks were up. Take the bass part to "Bad Moon Rising," I think it's not enough, I think it could have had a little more variation, but I played what John wanted.

But songs like "Suzie Q," "Tombstone Shadow," "Born on the Bayou," when a guy writes a song, you think about how you want the parts to go. That doesn't mean everybody in the band is going to play your part and not change it. Does that mean every note in Creedence came out of John? Well, I guess he had it in his head. But I remember "Run Through the Jungle," where I didn't play the same on any one take. I had to learn the part for touring from the record. Doug's contributions, like the cool drum stuff on "Who'll Stop the Rain," which makes that song, that's an instrumental hook. We could go on and on. That hurts more than a lot of the stuff, to read that we weren't any good. Hey, you could have dumped us any time, pal, and gone to studio cats like Buddy Holly did. Who in their right mind wouldn't give John credit for his role in the band? That'd be real revisionism. But why take the credit away from the guys who were actually there? (1998)

FROM WOODSTOCK TO
COSMO'S FACTORY

F or John Fogerty, Woodstock was the realization of the dream that took root when he imagined himself as the leader of Johnny Corvette and the Corvettes. "By the time we got to Woodstock, I felt we were the number one band," he recalled. "Assuming that the Beatles were God, I thought that we were the next thing under them, that our rocket ship was blazing through the sky hotter and higher and faster than anyone else's."

He wasn't altogether deluding himself. By 1969, Creedence Clearwater Revival had won a place in the highest echelon of the rock world. During the summer that reached its mythic apex at Yasgur's Farm, the group headlined major festivals in Newport, Denver, and Atlanta. Over the next three years, the string of top ten singles that began with "Proud Mary" and "Bad Moon Rising" continued with "Green River," "Down on the Corner," "Travelin' Band," "Up Around the Bend," and "Lookin' Out My Back Door." While Fogerty considered the hits fundamental, CCR also developed into a great album band with Green River, Willy and the Poor Boys, and Cosmo's Factory, each of which plays its distinctive variation on the swamp rock theme. When Fogerty created his mythic washtub band and included versions of Leadbelly's "Midnight Special" and "Cotton Fields" on Willy and the Poor Boys, *he was staking CCR's formal claim to a place in the American grain.*

At its peak, CCR reached an audience that encompassed hippies, bikers, counterculture intellectuals, rock-and-roll traditionalists, grunts trying to relax in the hooches and PXs of Vietnam, and a whole bunch of kids who couldn't have cared less about anything other than a good tune and a rockin' beat. "Green River," "Down on the Corner," and "Up Around the Bend" implied a vision of America as open and hopeful as anything created by Elvis, Chuck Berry, Buddy Holly, or Little Richard when rock and roll was just finding its voice.

And Fogerty forged that vision without denying any of the harsh blues truths about Vietnam-era America. "Fortunate Son" identifies the hypocrisy and violence underlying America's Fourth of July rhetoric as clearly as any political critique; the haunting image of a crowd huddled together trying to keep warm in "Who'll Stop the Rain" cuts to the desperation behind the communal dream. Almost everyone heard "Run Through the Jungle" as a nightmare vision of Vietnam, where "Satan cries 'take aim.'" But Fogerty had written the song about violence on the streets of our cities. Satan wasn't out there taking orders from Ho Chi Minh. He was right here in the heart of our own darkness.

CCR's music of the late sixties and early seventies raised the most difficult questions about what America was, what it is, what it might be. An unmistakable streak of fatalism ran through Fogerty's music. You could hear "Who'll Stop the Rain" as a rejection of political action, a weary dismissal of the myth that change was possible. But chances are you were listening to it right alongside "Fortunate Son," which could be, and was, heard as a call to action, an affirmation of the idea that, however battered and bruised we felt, we had a foundation on which to build a community to fight the hypocrisy and lies and violence.

It didn't work out that way, for America or for Creedence Clearwater Revival. The group continued to project its communal image and gave the idea physical form in the actual Cosmo's Factory, an Oakland warehouse converted into a hybrid recording studio, rehearsal space, and recreation center. But the pressures of the feverish pace of productivity—required by a contract that obligated Fogerty to deliver more than two dozen songs a year—were beginning to wear him down. Even at Woodstock, CCR's moment of symbolic arrival, there were indications of the problems to come.

Stu Cook

By the time we got [to Woodstock] the fences had come down and it was total chaos. Everyone's equipment was breaking, but, hey, it was the first time anyone had tried to do this. So problems were to be expected, weren't they? It had to be well after midnight. The Dead had played a long set, I don't even recall if it was a good Dead set or not a good Dead set, but it was late when we went on. There were monitor problems, and I think the bass wasn't even plugged in for the first song. (1998)

Doug Clifford

Woodstock was great except we had to follow the Grateful Dead. They played a forty-five-minute version of "Turn On Your Love Light." I was so uptight and so upset. They were supposed to play an hour. A good black group playing forty-five minutes is stretching it, but the Grateful Dead. . . . They basically put the audience to sleep; we had to try to bring them back. That was hard. (1998)

John Fogerty

We didn't actually do very well at Woodstock because of the time segment and also because we followed the Grateful Dead, therefore everybody was asleep. It's true. They put half a million people to sleep and in hindsight, since so many more people profess to having been at Woodstock, it's probably five million people. It seemed like we didn't go on till two o'clock in the morning. It was way later than we were supposed to go on. We were supposed to be in the prime spot for that evening. But it's an old story, the Dead went on and pulled their usual shenanigans. They tuned, like, for forty minutes and then they played a while and then all their equipment broke and it's, like, classical mythic Grateful Dead, and it seemed like an endless amount of intermission and guess what? They started playing again. So they were on the stage literally for two and a half hours, and we had to go on after that.

Not many people know this story, but after six straight songs of John and the band giving it all our energy and hoping we can win the day. . . . You look out and it's dark and you see all these people asleep and they're intertwined like muddy half-naked bodies, like pictures of souls coming out of Hell, and I look out there and I say into the microphone, "We're really having a great time up here, we hope you're having a good time too." And I look out and see all these mouths open and asleep. But one guy way way way out there flicks his lighter and he says, "Don't worry about it, John, we're with ya." And I played the whole rest of the show to that guy. It really is true. (1998)

Stu Cook

Actually, we played a hell of a show. I think we had one of the better sets of the whole three days, but John refused to have us involved in the soundtrack or the movie, which I think were big managerial mistakes, because everyone in that movie got their career launched to at least the next level. It would have been perfect for where we were. It was a decision John made and we had to chew on it. He told us we played a bad set and that's why we weren't in it. Well, we got four tunes on the boxed set, the twenty-fifth anniversary. I think we played well, John sang well. I don't understand, it was just a mistake. It's sad that we have to convince people we were there at the biggest musical event in our lifetimes. We shoulda been right there, side one, cut one. (1998)

John Fogerty

Even though in my mind we made the leap into superstardom that weekend, you'd never know it from the [film] footage. And that's why we don't show up on the album or in the film. It's a famous moment in Creedence history. Even though the other three wanted us to be in them [the movie and the album], I said no. All that does is show us in a poor light at a time when we were the number one band in the world. Why should we show ourselves that way? So I prevailed. (1998)

Doug Clifford

But being there and seeing all the people and the naked mud bodies. You could honestly feel the vibe there. That's corny and trite and cliché, but you could feel vibrations. It was awesome. You put half a million people together under the worst of conditions, no water, no food, no toilets, rain, no shelter. Two people died, two people were born. It was nonviolent. It'll never happen again, I'm afraid. It was heavenlike, what can I say? Just a very very neat thing. We weren't there long. We left after we played, but we were there long enough to know this was something very special. (1998)

By 1969, CCR's days of playing roadhouses and military bases were fading into memory. The group played the Newport '69 Pop Festival in Northridge, California, before an audience of 150,000; the Denver Pop Festival, which featured the last performance of the Jimi Hendrix Experience; the Atlantic City Pop

Overleaf: A calm moment in the studio, 1970 *(Courtesy Graham Niven)*

Festival; the Atlanta Pop Festival; and Woodstock. CCR frequently performed in support of political causes, playing a benefit at Shea Stadium in New York to raise campaign funds for candidates running on peace platforms, and another at the Fillmore West to raise funds for the Haight-Ashbury Medical Center heroin program. John Fogerty found himself contemplating his group's changing relationship with its audience.

John Fogerty

We want to reach everyone. Literally everyone. And that's why it's hard, because I'm not trying to polarize hippies against their parents, or youth against their parents, or youth against . . . just the people who are in their twenties, because there's a thing there now, too, or vice versa, you know— "We ain't no teenyboppers!" Because I think music, my concept of what music is supposed to be, shouldn't do that. It should unite, as corny as that is. You know, everyone should be able to sit and tap their foot, or say, "Wow! That's the right thing. I should have been thinking that, rather than. . . . " (1970)

It was obvious that something big was happening by the late part of 1969. That was always my dream. You can dream something. It doesn't mean you're not living in reality. If somebody comes down the street and says, "Come on, be real," you can do that too if you're not one of those crazy people. But you have your dream and your dream is full of great expectations. Hey, man, I wanted to be Elvis. By the time we got to Woodstock, I felt we were the number one band. Assuming that the Beatles were God, I thought that we were the next thing under them, that our rocket ship was blazing through the sky hotter and higher and faster than anyone else's. (1998)

Stu Cook

The Atlanta pop festival and the one in Newport, Southern California, were both great festivals. This is really weird, but we were being booked by an agency at the time and right after playing Woodstock for three quarters of a million people, the next day we played at a little tent in New Jersey for about five hundred people. It was like, "Wait a minute, what happened, what are we doing now?" It was scary. What I remember about the festivals most is that they never had enough toilets, they never had enough water, and they never figured out how to get the bands in and out when the roads got all jammed. That was the common thread between all festivals—and you were lucky if you got paid. We didn't get paid for a long time after Woodstock. (1998)

John Fogerty

I don't remember all the festivals in detail, but when someone mentions one it comes back. Like in Denver, I think the night before had been Jimi Hendrix, they had tear gas and a riot. And then Altamont slowed everything down. I really enjoyed the festivals. The kids were young and free and not expecting first-class treatment. I was a kid myself and very much a part of the audience. I remember the Atlanta Pop Festival. We mostly played the festivals in 1969; by 1970 we were in our own orbit and atmosphere. In Atlanta, I was very much taken by meeting B. B. King, who was forty-two years old. He looked great. He told us he'd never missed a gig and never been late for a gig and I was very much impressed by his workingman's ethic. (1998)

Stu Cook

The road? Hmmm—remember the circus? The excitement before television? For kids? Well, that's the road for us. What the circus used to be. You start in New York City and Memphis knows you're comin' and it just snowballs. Beautiful. And we don't want anything but for them to have a good time. See, we're paying them back for loving us. A concert is like making love: the play before, the act itself, and the satisfaction afterward. We pick the benefits we play carefully. Is it going to go any further than that one benefit we're playing? If it's gonna stop right after we leave the hall, forget it. (1971)

At the time, CCR's success prompted Fogerty to reconsider his relationship with success and with the music business.

John Fogerty

It's just who dictates taste. And if you're gonna go with the majority-dictated taste, then obviously, for them, *that's* right. That's the only split I have with commercialism as a word, meaning business, and commercialism meaning sound. They've come to mean two things now. There's nothing wrong with selling records—which is being commercial. The only thing I hate is that commercial sound. . . . Obviously, we're trying to be heard by as many people as possible. I can't picture an artist sitting in his room, a painter or whatever, thinking, "I don't want anyone to ever see what I do." You couldn't have your own id, you couldn't have a soul and not say, "Gee, I'd like to show this to somebody." And so if you set out saying, "Well, you know, I don't want anyone to . . . I don't want to be successful." Success means . . . I don't know how you would picture it, but to me success means a lot of people accepted what you do.

Therefore, you can tell a lot more people, you know, about the way you see the world. And to me, that's good. That's great. It gives you a platform. Especially if you've got your double-whammy thing way back there in your head, and someday you're going to bring it out, you can be successful first, and then say, "Here it is!" Which is what I think the Beatles did. A lot more people will listen. But success probably gets in the way sometimes.

I used to scream and rant and rave, really. I'd just tear people to pieces. And unduly so. I mean, I never realized they thought so much of me. There was a kid in Toronto, poor guy, there was an Electric Circus up there. The soundman wasn't there, and the promoter was a real schmuck, and I hate those kinds of guys, and it was that kind of a tour. Just guys that didn't have nothin' ready. So he just put this kid in there, you know. Twenty years old or somethin', the age doesn't make him a kid, it was just that *he'd* never done it before. So I said, "Put in a little bass." He turned the bass all the way on and the thing just started going *rgggh* and nobody could hear, and the sound was terrible, and the monitors were awful. I didn't chew him out, but I can be really sarcastic when I want to. But I didn't know he wasn't the right guy, and I also didn't realize we were as popular, especially with him, you know. He was looking at me like the way I look at Mick Jagger or Bob Dylan or somebody. . . . And for somebody like that—I just castrated him. And I didn't realize, you know, I was just a musician, I wasn't a star or anything in my head. I didn't know people were thinking that way. And so it was devastating. The poor kid was crying, and it was really just whap! But he was in the wrong position. I think I learned after that it wasn't fair. People expect more of me, even when it's wrong. I took the microphone and just jammed it into the speaker. The Who. That's what it was. But I was mad. I was really angry. Now, we've learned, it's happened so often, we've learned that there's nothing you can do. In those days we thought that there *was* something we could do. What we're gonna do now is produce our own shows. Then it'll be our fault anyway. So I have nobody to kick but myself.

We went on a little bit of a spree around "Proud Mary." We saw we were being successful; we could get things done we'd always wanted. I got a good tape recorder, a good record player. I got all this stuff and none of it worked. It was all junk. It was all the best names and everything. And it was just crap. And you send it back to get it fixed, and they don't fix it. We learned in about a month or so that it's really not important. That isn't what it's all about. That isn't what the top of the heap is. Or any of that crap. Take that away and we're still the same people, rich or poor. You still gotta learn what life is about. Say you fill this whole room with everything you ever wanted . . . a color TV, ninety-eight inches. And a brand-new Rolls Royce or something. Boy, you don't live in those things! I mean you gotta spend your life *doing* something. You can't ride around in your car and say, "Wow! What a wonderful life!" You gotta strip that all away and say, "Now what do I do? I'm bored." You can't let all that crap entertain you. You certainly can't look at your bank balance or something, and add it up twenty-seven times a day.

I guess I'd be kidding myself if I said that criticism doesn't bother me. It bothers me, but mostly it bothers me if they hit the wrong things. If they put me down for the wrong reasons, it really bothers me. If they get me on something, if they say, "He's not really that great a singer," or if they say, "Gee a lot of their songs are similar." That stuff doesn't bother me. Or if they say, "He isn't the world's greatest harp player," that doesn't bother me. I never said I was. But if they say, "Gee, they weren't communicating at all with the audience. They weren't liking it. They just got a ten-minute ovation." And some guy, he's sitting there, he was sittin' behind a post or somethin', couldn't see the show, and he didn't dig it, so he wrote that. Aw, c'mon, mister. Gimme a break! It's that kind of thing. And the same thing with praise. It weighs. It really does. It balances, because a lotta people rave over things that aren't that good. You know, "Oh, fantastic, fantastic guitar." I can't read any one article, I have to read a whole lot and then sort of take the average. Because if people are saying, "This is great!" and others are saying, "It's terrible!" you gotta figure, it's not either one. It's sort of in the middle.

I'm not sure just who really likes us the most. In the beginning I was a little worried, because we made it coincidentally on AM radio. To me, it was great. I mean, that proves that, not *proves*, but it's a sign at least, that you're getting past any of the corny lines that people draw, and it bugged me that a certain section of our society, probably where we came from really, were saying, "Gee, they're makin' it there. I don't like 'em." Hopefully that's going away because obviously—I hope it's obvious—that isn't what our interests are. Because I'd hate to have people not listen just because "I know what he's doing." To me, that's a drag. Which is the same reasoning, by the way, why we don't go around shouting, "Hey, legalize dope! Hey, peace now!" or something. All the time. I mean you can say it at the right moment, but if that's all you say. . . . As an entertainer to his audience, I don't want anyone just going, "I know what he's gonna say," and then not listen. You want 'em to listen, and especially if you're gonna say something that sort of reaches beyond normal entertainment, you know. We've got enough goin' against us just because we have long hair. There's a certain element won't listen anyway, which is a drag. (1970, 1971).

Rachel Donahue

In January 1970 we put on a Creedence concert at Oakland Alameda Coliseum; Tom [Donahue] was a promoter of note. We just did it because we liked them. And at this particular point, Al Jackson, Booker T. and the MGs' drummer sat in. They were doing a tape and John did a twenty-two-minute version of "In the Midnight Hour" and the guy ran out of tape about ten minutes into it and they wanted to hang themselves. (1998)

John Fogerty

There was a concert that was being taped as the pilot for the show that became known all through the seventies as "In Concert," the one Don Kirschner did. This was the pilot show, well in advance of when that thing got off the ground. We were the headline act and we called Booker T. and the MGs to be the opening act. They were huge idols to us. I still think that was the best rock-and-roll band of all time. In taping stuff around it, we had some footage of us all jamming. Al Jackson, Jr., and Doug were playing drums and Cropper's there, and I'm playing, Booker hadn't gotten there yet, but it was an intermingling of both our bands playing at the same time. It was really cool. There was some footage, but I haven't seen it for thirty years. (1998)

In 1970, CCR toured Europe for the first time. It was about that time that Fogerty decided that the group would no longer play encores. The decision marked a turning point in his relations with the rest of the band.

Stu Cook

We toured Europe once as a four-piece and once as a three-piece. They were pretty good times. Unfortunately, we got hooked up with this promoter who agreed to pay us X a night and he had people over there paying through the nose for tickets. We weren't getting any money, but every press conference we had, they'd just grill us about the economics of the tour. Which ultimately led to me mouthing off to *Rolling Stone* magazine and the band getting sued because of comments I made about slimy promoters. Me and my mouth again. But we just didn't have our eyes open. We signed those contracts. We stepped up for everything that happened to us. Some of us have been able to accept our mistakes, some don't want to acknowledge them. (1998)

John Fogerty

The first time we went overseas was in early 1970. We went to England, France, Germany, Sweden, Denmark. On the first tour, the reception was very wild. England was incredible. We played Albert Hall two nights. I had told the audience we didn't do encores, and I told them this would be our last number. I used to say that if the Beatles would give in, people would have them play encores for twenty-four hours. It was becoming a showbiz thing that wasn't very relevant to the superstar bands. So even though I said this would be our last song, we did "Chooglin'." We left and people kept shouting and applauding and everything for fifteen minutes. It caused quite a stir in England. They brought up the lights and they played "God Save the Queen" several times, but the people kept thinking we were coming back. One of the reviewers said we should learn about the music hall tradition in England, because you're supposed to come back when the people applaud, but that was right in the face of them, they were playing the song, that's over. (1998)

Stu Cook

We played a show somewhere in Nebraska or Kansas. We came back in, the audience is going crazy. Doug said, "Let's go back out." John said, "No, we're not going back out, we're not doing an encore, we're not ever doing encores any more." We looked at him like, "What are you talking about? This is real. This is not just your token encore." In John's mind, encores were phony. We're not phony, therefore we won't do encores. We weren't about doing half-ass encores. If people wanted one it was because we'd played our asses off, we weren't faking it. At that point Doug completely exploded on John. It stopped just short of head-bashing. It was a bad moment. I didn't understand it, still don't understand it. (1998)

Doug Clifford

It was in the Midwest somewhere, sometime in seventy. We were in a locker room, just this big massage table for big basketball players. We had an excellent set, one of our best shows. We knew it and the crowd was going nuts. What happened was Tom and Stu were sitting on the floor leaning up against these lockers drinking Pepsis because we didn't even have beer, bottles of Pepsi. I'm drinking one and I'm hyper, sky-high, full of adrenaline, I'm little and I'm wiry and I'm strong for my size. When you have the adrenaline rush, you hear about ladies picking cars up off of kids, and I'm real excited, and I say, "What's the encore?" He said, "We're not doing one."

I thought he was kidding. I said, "What are you gonna do, let 'em bleed out there?" We had three songs we'd do, and we'd pick one depending on what the crowd was doing. He said, "We're not doing one" and he's sitting on this table, and I say, "Why? Why?" He says, "Encores are phony. From this moment on Creedence Clearwater will never do another one." I looked at Tom and Stu and said, "Let's go, guys, if we go out there he has to follow us. If we got out there, he's not gonna not show up. Let's go out." I start to go out and both of them put their heads down at the same time.

At that instant everything started going in slow motion for me. I went blank, all I could see was red. I couldn't see any image for about a second and I took the goddamn bottle of Pepsi and I smashed it against the locker as hard as I could. It shattered into a million pieces. I walked over to the table where John was sitting. The legs were wide. I picked the table up, and as I did the table tipped from his weight, he rolled off and things are in very slow motion and he rolled two and a half times and he rolled up against the locker. And he's looking at me and he's got his hands up like I was gonna crush him with the table. Now I've got the table up above my head and he's got his hands like he thinks I'm gonna throw the table on him, which would have

Cosmo on congas *(Courtesy Graham Niven)*

hurt him very seriously. And when I looked at him in the face, I looked him right in the eye, it was like the first day I ever met him, like he was thirteen years old again. And I broke the legs off the table and I pointed them at him and I said, "You're wrong, you're wrong," and I walked out. I wouldn't ride home with the band. So the next day I walked in and I said, "No more encores, we're having beer in the dressing room. No beer before the show, but you have your way, I'm having beer." We got beer, but we lost. That was the beginning of the end of the band, because we would go out and work the audience up and leave the stage knowing we couldn't do an encore and that was torturous. We never did one ever again. (1998)

The foundation of CCR's success remained its records. In 1996, Rolling Stone gave Willy and the Poor Boys *a place on its list of the best hundred albums of the rock-and-roll era, but an equally strong argument could be made for* Green River, *which remains the best expression of the group's communal myth. Even at the time, John Fogerty had a clear vision of the shape of CCR's career.*

John Fogerty

A single means you've got to get it across in a very few minutes. You don't have twenty minutes on each side of an LP. All it really means is you've got to think a little harder about what you're doing. We learned from the singles market not to put a bunch of padding on your album. Each song's got to go someplace. Most of this [backlash against singles] is a built-in uptightness: "Singles is what I dug when I was little, therefore I have to change now. I've grown up, I don't like Top Forty," which is dumb. Why not change Top Forty? (1970)

"Green River" didn't sound like "Proud Mary." The next single was "Down on the Corner" and "Fortunate Son." That didn't sound like "Green River." It was a change. I get very bored with people who would do the same musical thing over and over and just change a word here and there. I only wish that certain political things unrelated to music hadn't happened, because there would have been twenty more [singles]. I'd waited from the time I was going to be Johnny Corvette and the Corvettes. I had waited and learned and trained and exposed myself to influences, and when it was time to pop, I was ready.

My favorite album is *Green River,* and the older I get the more favorite, for a lot of reasons. Lately I've been playing dobro a lot and that dobro on the cover [of *Green River*] had sat on the shelf for more than twenty years. Somehow I not only connected with my own past going back to when I was six but I also predicted my future musically. It's sort of one long thing. It almost doesn't have time. "Bad Moon Rising," "Green River," that's the soul of where I live musically, the closest to what's in my heart. (1997)

As good as those records are, there's not a lot of technique there. Which is why they sound so good played by garage bands. And also, I might say, that's the same secret of Creedence. All the arrangements I did were for four people who were kind of medium talent or less on their instruments. So the reason all the Creedence stuff sounds so good by every bar band in the world is that the ability required to play the stuff is so minimal that anyone can play it and it sounds good. I still play in concert these days in a very simple way—not a lot of technique, not real complicated. My way of playing guitar is more like singing with the guitar, like a vocalist, so that you could hum the parts . . . everybody knows what you're doing. You can sing the guitar line; you can say it with your mouth. . . . So in the old days of Creedence, my aesthetic was more toward less is more, that simple is more powerful. I still feel that way. And I'm very happy with most of the stuff I did with Creedence. (1997)

Nothing is forced. If something doesn't hold up by itself, we won't do it till it feels completely comfortable. The relationship between all of us in the band gets better and better. We know ourselves. If somebody gets in a bad mood, we just leave him alone. We don't pick on each other. (1970)

The cover of Willy and the Poor Boys, *featuring CCR as a street band playing the traditional instruments described in "Down on the Corner," became a central part of the group's mythic image.*

John Fogerty

All the mythology, the choice of songs all came from John Fogerty. That was the world I lived in and still do. The musical choices and influences

FANTASY 8397

CREEDENCE CLEARWATER REVIVAL

DUCK KEE MARKET

ER WINE FROZEN FOOD PRODUCE MEAT

TON'S

WILLY AND THE POOR BOYS

were influences on me. I think it's obvious the way my career has gone that that fits perfectly with John, you can see my personality thirty years ago. The other guys weren't really into that stuff. I had grown up with a very musical mom. The folk music thing was something I was very much a part of. I went to lectures and forums, so I knew who all the old musicians were and had met a lot of them and people like Alan Lomax. So I was taking all of that in and it came out in *Willy and the Poor Boys*. In a loose Americana way it was kind of a tribute to them. I didn't have it all worked out, but I was thinking in those terms. I wrote the song first, "Down on the Corner," and peopled it with those guys Willy, Blinky, Rooster. They were kind of cartoonish characters and I made a little washboard band and then I chose to take [the cover] picture that reflected the song. I thought it was a very clear image, a good solid image. You didn't have to work real hard to get what the guy was talking about. I wanted to take a picture that looked like what the song was. With hindsight, you can see that John the PR guy was working overtime. There was no money, we didn't have Columbia Records putting out nine billion posters in every mall across the country. I used to say way back in 1968, "We don't have any money, so we're going to have to overcome them with ideas." If you have a strong idea, it's worth a million dollars. (1998)

Stu Cook

We were going to shoot the album cover and the idea was Willy, John, on harmonica, and the poor boys, Doug, Tom, and myself, and we had our instruments. Doug had a washboard, which is a traditional American instrument, and I had the gut bass. My dad taught me how to play the gut-bucket, one string bass on a broom handle on a galvanized metal tub. You play it with a big leather glove so you don't tear up your hand.

[The cover photo] was an accident. It was such a chaotic session, the guy ran out of film or something and we were just standing around and all these kids jumped in and started goofing around with us. John's got the harmonica and Doug's got the washboard and I'm thumping away on the gutbucket and Tom's strumming on this crappy acoustic guitar we have almost as a prop. And these kids start freaking out and the guy who was still there had a couple of shots left when he sent his partner off to get more film, just popped off a few shots that just seemed to have the best vibe. (1997, 1998)

As Creedence Clearwater Revival's visibility increased, John Fogerty found himself answering questions concerning his political beliefs and actions. As compared to many of their contemporaries, CCR avoided explicit ideological statements. Yet the music was a constant presence in activist circles. CCR's sound provided inspiration and energy to many determined to realize their own version of the democratic ideal.

John Fogerty

I really do feel strongly about a lot of this garbage that's happening today. I don't know what I can do about it yet. I want to get into the position where, when you say things people will listen, rather than, "Aw, we heard you before," you know. I want to be able to really, even with the money that we'll be able to generate on our own, take care of some of the things that I think are pretty simple, that *could* be simply taken care of now, or start to. No one seems to be *starting* yet. They're all talking.

I don't mean huge things that'll take generations, because maybe I can be one more cog in the wheel that'll help that. But there are so many simple things that could be done. And then I'll cop out and say I don't know what they are. But maybe [creating radio] stations like KPFA, or maybe even stronger than that, more outspoken, if that's possible. Papers not quite so weird as the *Berkeley Barb*, but papers for people that really read. Also raising money, which is so important all the time. I do know we're in a position where we can reach out just beyond the bounds of entertainment, of people looking and watching and saying, "Gee, see the clown dance," you know.

I think the reason I don't talk about it much is because I hear other people say it, and it sounds really insincere, like that's the thing you're supposed to say nowadays. I try to write songs and I can't get to it. The way, say, [TV newsman] Eric Sevareid seems to know every day exactly what's happenin'. And it just seems to me that if you could finally say it, to where enough people could finally see it the right way, that would solve half the problem. I think enough people just don't think, because it's not there in front of them, what's wrong. But you can see it now with the Moratorium [against the Vietnam war]. It's become so confused that now it's a choice of a bigger war or no war, rather than what the initial thing was all about. In other words, we've been given the spotlight or the center of the stage, and also the ability to raise money. I'm not hung up on money or any-thing, but everything costs so much just to do anything. It really does. People can't figure out why we're not out on the street with a sign—when we reach a million people with a record. It's like in the army, when you dig your last ditch. You hope you'll never have to use it. But if the time comes when we're pushed to our last ditch, damn straight we'll be out there in the street.

I'm afraid people really haven't listened to our words. They just think it's good-time music only: "Aren't you ever going to write anything that means anything?" That kind of bit, people ask all the time. And you have to talk back to them on their level. Because they haven't heard. People put too much weight on political references in songs. They think a song will save the world. That's absurd. (1970, 1971)

Power is the most correct word in the human language—and the most misunderstood. Power—two things. What they give you and what you give them. Hitler even beats the presidents, I guess. He had the most power recently. There's never going to be a time when the whole world—when everyone has the same powers. So the second best thing is to hap-pily make individuals use their own wills. I have power, sure. Nixon has. The pope. Muhammad Ali. All the same thing in varying degrees. Who takes politics seriously? Who takes religion seriously? Who takes boxing seriously? And who takes rock stars seriously? There's your answer. (1971)

On a concrete level, CCR provided financial support for the American Indian Movement during its occupation of Alcatraz Island. AIM activists LaNada Boyer and Edward Castillo remembered the group's contributions.

John Fogerty

For as long as the Indians continue to hold on, we'll support them. And

I hope that's gonna be a long, long time. (1971)

LaNada Boyer

When the government blocked our water barge and boats from docking on the island, Richard [Oakes] successfully brought in food and provisions on the opposite side of the island, where it was impossible to dock because of the high cliffs. When the government took the water barge away, we brought water over in a boat that Creedence Clearwater Revival bought for us. They bought the boat from Captain Cliff, whom we hired to take us back and forth from the mainland to the island. We named our boat the *Clearwater.* (1997)

Edward Castillo

We now were deluged with numerous supporters and supplies and a growing river of funds. Within a few weeks, John Fogerty, of the popular rock group Creedence Clearwater Revival, donated a fishing boat to the island's growing population. The press and media reports were becoming more analytical and were beginning to explore the conditions of Indian peoples nationwide. We were delighted that our demonstration had triggered some significant national reflections on the status of American Indians within American society. (1997)

Stu Cook

The band supported the American Indian Movement one hundred percent. We took the money out of our bank account and put it through another party and purchased the boat, but it was our doing. We supplied them with provisions to stay out there. Ultimately, what happened was, the Indians who were there, like Adam Fortunate Eagle, who lives near me in Nevada and has written a book on Alcatraz . . . he's convinced the Navy Seals sunk the boat to end the holdout. Because as long as they could reprovision, it coulda been a long stay. But as soon as the boat was sunk, they lost the ability.

It was our money, but we intentionally kept it quiet. You can align yourself with this cause and that cause and it's like doing benefits for everybody. You do this cause and you do that cause and pretty soon it doesn't mean anything, but you end up with all the baggage. We preferred to do things behind the scenes. All four of us were committed to the Indians. It wasn't really expensive, it might have cost us ten or fifteen grand, but back then it was a lot of money. What AIM did was an incredibly bold thing. What they did was needed to call attention, to rally and unite. (1998)

But without question, the real core of CCR's political presence came from the power of songs like "Fortunate Son" and "Run Through the Jungle."

John Fogerty

When I wrote "Fortunate Son," Julie Nixon was hanging around with David Eisenhower. And you just had the feeling that none of those people were going to be involved with the war. In 1969, the majority of the country thought morale was great among the troops, and like eighty percent of them were in favor of the war. But to some of us who were watching closely, we just knew we were headed for trouble. Some of the things I write, I'm sure people don't agree with. But I manage sometimes to be, purposely, like in the middle. Not because I'm coppin' out, but because there's things on both sides that're wrong. A song like "Fortunate Son," I'm sure a right-wing fool could take that as his rallying cry the same way. Because he doesn't agree with a lot of the things either, you know. To him, Richard Nixon ain't on his side at all. That kind of thing. It was written, of course, during the Nixon era, and, well, let's say I was very nonsupportive of Mr. Nixon. There just seemed to be this trickle down to the offspring of people like him. You got the impression that these people got preferential treatment, and the whole idea of being born wealthy or being born powerful seemed to really be coming to the fore in the late-sixties' confrontation of cultures. I was twenty-three years old, I think. I was mad at the specter of the ordinary kid who had to serve in an army in a war that he was very much against. Yet the sons of the well-to-do and powerful didn't have to worry about those things. They were fortunate. I thought all these guys were running around saying, "It's good for America"—Nixon or whoever was saying this. Yet their kids ain't going. (1971, 1993, 1997)

Stu Cook

We got tons of fan mail from Vietnam. Guys would send us stuff. I remember one real clearly, I think they were marines, sent us a picture standing around their tank and the name of the tank was "Proud Mary." There was the whole tank crew, guys with their shirts off. We felt like we were doing something helping there even though we weren't there. I really identify with the vets, even though it wasn't something I experienced.

And at the same time, we had a presence with the antiwar movement. We were of that age, activism was just starting to become a thing about my sophomore year in college. I remember being in a fraternity and we'd have endless, endless conversations, arguments about the war and the government. Finally, their arguments made more sense than the ones I was putting forth. I crossed the line then in terms of my attitude about the government and its direction. That would have been sixty-five, sixty-six, when we were just starting to get bogged down out there. The Kennedy legacy. (1998)

Doug Clifford

Several songs were written about our connection with the guys in the service. John was in the army reserve and he saw the inequities of the lower class and the middle class going while the privileged class didn't have to. That's what "Fortunate Son" is all about. It's written for the poor guys who got drafted over there and basically exposing those that didn't, the Dan Quayles of the world. "Who'll Stop the Rain" was about the Nixon administration, basically the reign of terror he was putting on the youth of America of having to go fight this war that was a corrupt war. A lot of people were making millions of dollars off that war basically on young blood.

We were very much aware and we supported the guys and we knew what it was like to be in the military and be forced to do what you didn't want to do. We didn't look at them like some of our peers and call them pigs and baby killers. The poor bastards were guys our age who were going over there and getting their asses shot off. Our heart was with 'em. It wasn't them, it was the administration, the Nixon administration. Kennedy basically got us in there, but it escalated under Johnson and Nixon. They were lying to the American people.

It was an issue where it took a lot of balls to stand up. A lot of guys called us long-haired cowards. But military guys loved us. A lot of them said, "Hey you got us through Vietnam." My answer to that was, "No, you got yourself through. We might have helped you a little bit. But we were behind you a hundred percent and we still are today." People don't realize unless they've been in the military what it's really like. These guys put their lives on the line. (1998)

John Fogerty

"Run Through the Jungle" was really about American society. It's funny that it got adopted by guys, they weren't really vets yet, they were grunts. After you got back you were a vet, but when you were over there you were "in country." The song was really my remark about American society, the metaphor being a jungle.

When I sang "two hundred million guns are loaded," I was talking about the ease with which guns are purchased in America. It was a jungle, and it's even worse now. To me, it's a sad thing. My commentary was "this isn't a good thing, two hundred million guns are loaded, Satan cries, 'Take aim.'" We're all killing each other. It's no different now. That part of it was an antigun statement. Now you may think it's a paradox because I'm a hunter. I love to go hunting. I enjoy the ownership of guns. Guns have a history and a lore just like guitars and cars and even women. But I'm not confused. I don't need an AK 47 to go deer hunting. It's pretty clear that if you have something like that, you want to kill people. Where if you go deer hunting, you want one shot. You can waste a lot of time with a hunting rifle on the machinery and all that. It's a lore thing. Or you can get a gun like old Wild Bill had, an old Colt six-shooter, a peacemaker. You can get all into that and that's cool. It's kind of American history and lore. The guy that buys a hunting license can feel that way. I think it's still respectable. But a person who buys an AK 47 is going to go rob a bank or wants to go kill somebody. Not necessarily so, he might just be a gun freak, but I don't think any true gun freak would mind being regulated. I think it's the nut cases that are bothered by that. Charlton Heston scares the shit out of me. Don't get me wrong, I'm a hunter and a lot of the NRA guys are hunters, but the NRA itself hasn't done the country any good with its endorsements of Teflon bullets, which were only meant to go through armored plate and kill policemen. I nailed it pretty good in "Violence Is Golden" [from the 1986 *Eye of the Zombie* album]. (1997)

The last of CCR's indisputably major albums, Cosmo's Factory *shifted the spotlight momentarily from John Fogerty to drummer Doug "Cosmo" Clifford. The album was named in honor of Clifford and of Cosmo's Factory, the group's rehearsal space. A converted warehouse, with a small carpeted recording studio, the Factory also featured a basketball hoop, a Ping-Pong table, a pool table, and an upstairs business office decorated with CCR posters, photos, and the band's numerous gold and platinum records. Factory had had a predecessor in the band's early days.*

Doug Clifford

It was a little shed in my backyard in a rented house in El Cerrito. We couldn't play in Tom's garage anymore because the neighbors'd call the police. We were working on the first album in there. It was a room maybe fifteen feet long and maybe eight feet wide and we put rugs over the doors and the windows. I was the only guy in the band who didn't smoke cigarettes—it drove me nuts. We'd be in there practicing with all the doors and windows shut so we wouldn't disturb the neighbors. At one point I got up and I said, "I gotta get outside, I can't even breathe in here, this is awful." Tom said, "Yeah, but it's better than working in a factory somewhere." The next day when the guys showed up for work, I'd painted on the door "The Factory." That was the first Cosmo's Factory.

Then, when got our warehouse, which became our headquarters in Berkeley, it was affectionately called Cosmo's Factory. It was a rehearsal space and we had our offices there. It was very funky. It was a manufacturing place that had stairs, and the upper level wasn't enclosed, it just had a railing that went all around it, it was all open. We had an area in the back that was curtained off, we had a rug and put in wall-to-wall carpet for our rehearsal area. Underneath it was the coffee machine and the main office was upstairs with the pool table and that sort of thing. (1998)

Stu Cook

Cosmo's Factory's just a big old warehouse down in the warehouse district of Berkeley, pretty close to the freeway, pretty close to the racetrack. My dad was a corporate attorney, civil attorney, and one of his clients was this contractor who just happened to own this building that was vacant. So we took a lease on it, it had two or three lofts. We put in a basketball court, draped the back, and that's where the *Cosmo's Factory* album cover was shot.

Since Doug was Cosmo, when we moved to the other place, it just became Cosmo's Factory. I think that was sixty-nine. The business had just moved up. We could afford a lease, a place we could drive our cars into it, roll up the doors. That was our spaceship for the rocket ride. The only people there were us and our employees: We had two road guys—Ray Francoise and Bruce Kourtz. We had a lighting guy, John. Jake Rohrer and, later, Mary Rohrer. Bruce Young worked with us.

It was like a family, we'd known a lot of people a long time. It added to the myth that we were not quite a hippie thing, but it had a communal vibe to it. There was nobody who came and hung around. Not much of anyone knew we were there. The rehearsal space was way in the back so you could barely hear it outside. The back of the warehouse abutted another warehouse and it was a foundry, and when they'd fire up those forges and the metal you had to turn up 'cause it would drown you out. (1998)

Doug Clifford

If John had been a little more relaxed and given Tom some space to take some pressure off of him, it might have been different. That's what *Cosmo's Factory* was all about. I was the outgoing guy, the guy who was real comfortable with people. I could get up on a stage right now in front of a thousand people and tell jokes and be perfectly comfortable. He wasn't comfortable with people and the press and that was when the pressure was mounting. And, he says, we're naming this after you and the press is gonna be all over you wanting to know why, so I need you to take the pressure off me. I said, I'd love to, I'm gonna have fun with it. I told them a different story every city we went to. It was the greatest rock-and-roll band in the world. For a four-piece guitar band, we were the best America ever produced. (1998)

Stu Cook

The album *Cosmo's Factory* was really a collection of singles. That album was recorded over ten months. We'd just go in and record A and B sides, release it, A and B sides, release it, and we had over half the album done before we went in to do "Grapevine" and the cover tunes, "Oooby Dooby," whatever else. The singles were out there already because we were working at this breakneck pace so we wouldn't fall off the planet.

On *Cosmo's Factory*, there was not a lot of musical growth, not a lot of forward or upward movement. There was a lot of exploring other areas. We did more country music, country-flavored stuff, and explored other areas and styles. But it was still basically two guitars, bass, and drums. So we were able to record that album in two or three weeks' time. (1997, 1998)

John Fogerty

Green River's probably my favorite, I like where that music is, the sound of it, the cover, everything. But as far as the best record, I would imagine *Cosmo's Factory.* I always considered that kind of the culmination. I always thought that's what it was. Creedence had these records and we put everything on it. It was almost like redemptive, you might say. Boom, there I said it again.

My favorite songs on the album are probably "Who'll Stop the Rain," and I really like "Lookin' Out My Back Door." We went in to record it, and I liked it when I wrote it, and then I forgot about it. Then I heard it a few weeks later, and I heard it again, and it was like hearing it for the first time all over, and I thought to myself, "Gee, that's a nice song." (1997)

Cosmo's Factory *marked the end of one of the most intensely creative periods any rock band ever experienced. By the end of 1970, however, the strains had begun to affect the band. Responding to group members' feelings that the band wasn't as highly recognized as it should be given the popularity of its records, and increasingly angry at Fantasy's inadequate promotion, the band hosted a huge industry party on December 12, 1970, flying in critics and industry figures from around the country. Expressing the band's consensus, Stu Cook recalled, "I don't think Fantasy ever bought an ad for us. That big party we threw, most people think that was a Fantasy party. We paid for every penny of that." By the start of 1971, tensions between Fantasy and CCR had reached an explosive point. While the eventual blowup centered on Zaentz and John Fogerty, Cook and*

Clifford shared John's belief that Fantasy had failed to give the group the respect or remuneration it deserved. While everyone agrees that, in Cook's words, "we got screwed," Cook and Clifford believe Fogerty has not fully accepted his part of the responsibility for what took place.

Doug Clifford

It pisses me off good. We're worth more than just a "ho-hum, another hit from Creedence" attitude. We have something to say and we want to say it. Everyone has the most fucking respect for the Beatles. Well, we're the biggest American group. We put out quality records. We go over and over our songs. We rehearse hours, every day. Nothing bad gets out under our name. We have artistic control. We even carry our own sound system. We shouldn't be taken lightly, barked at. You can't sell that many records and be taken lightly. (1970)

Stu Cook

Your career doesn't go to the place it's supposed to unless every area is used. People know about our music, but they don't know about our heads. We're tired of that riff about John Fogerty's backup band. That's all changed now, anyway. For a long time we just stepped out of the way and let John run the group, but about three months ago that changed. We all contribute now. All of us play other instruments and now we're going to start doing that in the act. That frees John. He was manager, leader—now he can play piano and organ as well as guitar and songwriting and singing. The Beatles moved from nowhere to somewhere. That's the way you have to do it. We'd like to change people's heads to an understanding that we can't be used by the extremes of either side, that we are interested in social causes but aren't willing to go far left to prove it.

CCR at Forest Hills, New York, 1971 *(Dagmar/Star File)*

People forget that rock is a part of show business, just like the theater. It's your audience—they come to see you and to be entertained. If they like you, they'll find out who you are. Groups like Led Zeppelin and ourselves have made it primarily on the strength of live appearances and record sales. I'm sure the success of our appearances in London had a lot to do with us being voted the top group by readers of the *New Musical Express* there—over the Beatles, who had topped that poll for years. Plus the fact that we sell a tremendous amount of singles as well as albums. Our only identification has been through having our faces on our album covers and magazine coverage. I guess nearly everyone in the world has heard of the Beatles . . . and at least half of them must know each one by name. At first people were hardly conscious of Beatles music. It was the individual personalities that they were digging. It was all so very new and the publicity machine was geared to handle it. When they first broke in America the Beatles were quite unique and were definitely the first shining light in rock music for over five years. (1971)

When "Bad Moon Rising" went number one in England, we had a little party down at Fantasy. That was pretty good for us. We thought, it's not just here, it's overseas. For us to be number one in the country of the Stones and the Beatles, that was really something. Doug and I went out and got in a huge wreck about an hour after that celebration. His Porsche was totaled, my motorcycle was totaled.

Pop music was different then. Rock music was a spotty little upstart. It had come a long way from Fats and Ricky and Elvis. We were kind of the third wave. The British came through with the Beatles, the Stones. We invigorated Americans, kind of got back into it with our own music again. It didn't surprise me that Diana Ross would have a number one single instead of us. There were just more people listening to pop music, and on top of that Motown was spending money. Fantasy never did. (1998)

Tom Fogerty

The record business is the fastest-moving business of them all. Last Friday was last Friday. What we may have been thinking then has changed by Monday. It has to. Yeah, true art is good a hundred years later, but I don't think true artists went around saying that. They just did it. (1971)

John Fogerty

Well, I know on the one hand that the critics don't buy many records, and I don't like things force-fed, so this whole thing is a concession in a way. We've always felt that you don't need all the jive that people go through. But on the other hand, Fantasy never had that much money to spend on us when we were new, and we did it without all the hype. But unfortunately, I think the critics somehow believe the hype. We always thought you could appeal to people's common sense and intelligence, but that isn't the way it works out. The Beatles had a lot of hype, but their music was cool so it was worth it. I've made compromises with myself. (1970)

Saul Zaentz

There's a lot of bullshit in the record business. Why them? All you can go on is what you feel. I liked their music. But the money we've spent promoting people who never make it—all those Jims and Johnnys and Joes and Jeffs. Nobody writes about them. Record people always say, "Nothing will sell." And ninety-three percent of the time they're right. Sure, the distributors are in it for the money. What else? If records didn't sell, they'd be selling shirts. The word "fan" comes from fanatic. Creedence Clearwater don't just reach fans—they reach married couples too. The only one I can compare them to, for selling records, is Elvis, back in the fifties. To maintain it the way they have. They were the biggest sellers in the world. Next to the Beatles and above the Rolling Stones in sales. Because they hit another field—a pop field—where the Rolling Stones were a bit more esoteric at the time. They reached a big pop market. (1971, 1998)

Stu Cook

We got screwed. The bottom line is, [Fantasy] reneged. They don't see it that way. But [screwed] in the spirit of the deal when we sat at Saul's house and signed with him and he agreed to buy John a lead guitar amplifier, which he desperately needed. We needed a good deep sound.

Even if we didn't play psychedelic music like the rest of the bands, we played long blues solos, which is really what psychedelic music is, white guys playing blues. We were flat-ass broke. So we sat in Saul's kitchen in Kensington, California, this is before the first album, right after he bought the company, after we changed our name. He said, "When you guys hit it, you're equally in the pie." And we never got anything. We did get a raise where they gave us some tidbits. They raised the price of the product, though. We still have the most pathetic domestic royalty rate of any artists living.

Stu Cook at work *(Courtesy Graham Niven)*

Our singles never made number one because they didn't play the game, they didn't market. In those days it was little Fantasy against RCA, Capitol, Columbia, who signed all the other artists in the Bay Area: Jefferson Airplane, Steve Miller Band, Moby Grape, Sly and the Family Stone, Santana. That's how you play the game, how artists get into the Hall of Fame. All of these awards are set up for the companies that spend the money. The number one single is the same. I've seen it happen in country music all the time, the publishers sit around in Nashville and decide who's going to have the number one song. There's three, four, five big publishing houses and they just trade it back and forth.

After Tom had left we were finally able to negotiate a little bit better deal, and that's when we got the deal we have now, which I described as the worst. The one before it was even worse. We've gone back to Fantasy every three or four years and said, "Come on, man, we're still selling two million units a year, why don't you give us something that approaches what a new act would get today?" We're not even asking for what the Doors are getting today, Jimi Hendrix, just what a new act would get. They say, "No, man, you're a band of the sixties, we've got a contract, we'll live with it."

But, hey, I gotta do business with them. I don't have to sue to get my money. What's the point? Am I just going to drag this around like the baby ghost with the ball and chain? Life is not meant to do that. We were young, we were dumb. We signed a bad contract without any advice. John was our manager. Someday some of this has got to come back to John. I have never ever seen John take any responsibility. He wants all the credit, but he will never take one lick of responsibility. (1998)

Signs of the band's internal problems had begun to emerge by the end of 1970. Still, the group viewed Cosmo's Factory as a place where it could work through the problems and stay together.

John Fogerty

After rehearsing [at Cosmo's Factory] for some time, we took a close look at the place and decided that we could easily fix it up and it would make a great headquarters for during the day.

You gotta make the effort [to stay together]. You really do. It's not an effort to like each other, but if you got any sense at all, you realize that everybody has bad days. And if all four of us have one the same day, it could be hell. It really could. We've had times when we scream at each other. It's nothing like it was when we were little kids. One day Doug said, "I'm checking my gear." He was gonna pack 'em off about something. And we play little games with each other. The next day everything was fine again . . . me and Stu got together, and we said, "We're gonna kick you out. We found this other drummer." And just hurt [Doug's] mind a little. But we know nothing like that's gonna happen. It never even enters into it. It's the same with a wife or with a family. You can have the knock-downest, drag-outest argument you can think of, but the question of divorce never enters your mind. That's not the weapon you use. Which is the same with the band. The only thing we ever hassle over is the music. "It sounded a certain way." "Well, I don't like it." And we all sort of have accepted that I am the leader in that respect. You know there's gotta be one voice; otherwise, you just . . . you never get anywhere. We all talk and we all listen, and then we just sort of . . . we don't even vote. We just say, "Well, what do ya think?" Well, it isn't that big a deal. If we don't do it then—whatever they want—well then, we'll do it later. In the long run, the only thing that's important to us, really, is our career and staying together. And so, therefore, we try to eliminate all the things that might jeopardize that. (1971)

Stu Cook

After many years of continued hardship and struggling, you really get to know who your friends are. Everyone on our payroll is just that, a good friend. Musicianwise we may not be the best band in the world, but togetherwise we've got every one of them licked. It's just like the hare and the tortoise. There is much more to show business than talent. (1971)

Doug Clifford

It's the same within the group. In a lifetime you are lucky to have one true and honest friend. I have three. We were friends long before we became a band, and personally I think that's why we eventually made it. As friends we continually help each other. (1971)

Stu Cook

The band started as a real dreamy kind of communal thing because all of us had to pull together to survive economically. We sold our assets, Tom took his retirement fund, and we were living on twenty dollars a week. So we had to care about each other and help. When somebody needed something, the rest of us did without. It was real. There's no other way it can feel for me. Those were the things that really happened. Everybody in the band gave a hundred and ten percent. It may have been John's swampy bluesy vision, but we were the people who materialized the dream, we gave it the flesh and the bone. (1998)

JOHN FOGERTY, SONGWRITER

W hatever the complications surrounding the myth and history of Creedence Clearwater Revival, one thing is certain: John Fogerty has earned a place in the pantheon of American vernacular songwriters that includes Bob Dylan, Bruce Springsteen, gospel pioneer Thomas Dorsey, and bluesmaster Willie Dixon. Reflecting on the approach to songwriting that produced "Proud Mary," "Bad Moon Rising," and "Who'll Stop the Rain" along with less well-known masterpieces such as "Wrote a Song for Everyone" and "It Came out of the Sky," Fogerty described a conscious effort to link personal, political, and mythic meanings.

John Fogerty

I used to use the word "biblical" [to describe his awareness of CCR's myth]. When I would write a song like "Who'll Stop the Rain" I made it general and epochal. I tried to stretch it and make it bigger so that it wasn't just a song about me, so that lots of other people could look into the song and see themselves in it too. I did that on purpose. I was the opposite of somebody like Joni Mitchell, who would write these very personal songs and then hope that everyone else would relate to it that way, as if the person were them. I tended to make the song very broad and hope that lots of people would see it that way. (1998)

In the course of a probing interview with Ralph Gleason that provided the core of a 1970 Rolling Stone *cover story, Fogerty provided his first extensive commentary on his songwriting process.*

John Fogerty

[I write songs] with the guitar, usually . . . mostly without anything, riding along in the car or a lot of times I just lay in bed at night and think for two or three hours, you know. But I make all the noises, like with the drums, and that really helps, it really does. In fact, I usually base everything on drum and bass riffs. I'll get the beat going first, and then I'll picture the melody. Up till now I've had no place where I could let loose and sing loud. The neighbors'd complain or something. Now I'm building my little place in my house so I'll be able to do that. I don't know whether there'll be a difference or not.

Then on the other hand, for the real beef of the song, and what it's going to be about, the words and everything, I kinda do that separately—sometimes before, sometimes after. And then I sort of put them together. Like I have, well, a little notebook full of titles, full of one-liners that can either be a title or part of a song, that sort of thing. In fact, the first page, you know, I really had a streak, and the first page had . . . "Proud Mary" was the first thing on it, and somewhere in the middle was "Lodi," "Bad Moon Rising," and near the end was something called "Riverboat" and "Rolling on the River." It came out to be "Proud Mary." If I had it all written down, it would have been too manufactured. Originally there were three separate things. Eventually they got together and became "Proud Mary." I didn't conceive of "Proud Mary" as a boat at all. I was thinking of a washerwoman or something. It's completely different.

Some writers have huge, organized files of lyrics and titles. I can't do that. The creative process, I've found, is extremely unorganized. I might have just a title, "Penthouse Pauper," but no matter how I try I can't write it. It can't be forced. It's a waste of time to force it. I'm better off spending the time practicing my open E chord. I have to be relaxed in order to write. I can't come in from the boxing match of daily living and start writing, unless I want to write a protest song. . . . I want to perfect my writing. I'd like to be able to say something that needs thirty words but break it down to two words.

I never finished a song that I won't use. In fact, in our career so far, I think we've thrown away, since Creedence I mean, I think we've thrown away one song per album, except the last one. We used everything we intended to use . . . this is the brand new one. The first album we were ever gonna have, we did, I think a Bo Diddley song which didn't work out. And I kept telling myself, "Now if we were the Beatles, we wouldn't use that because it's no good." And we came up to the final thing, and I thought, "Oh well, what the heck, if they can throw it away, we'll throw it away, too." And that's the way it worked out. I guess I've written around two hundred songs. That's in the last four years. When I was really young I probably wrote, I couldn't count, maybe five hundred. It seemed like zillions to me. They were all garbage, really. Every one of them was the same thing, unrequited love. Which is why I can't write about that stuff now too much. If I'm going to write a love song, or anything dealing with that, it's either gotta be very real or just camp, a good old rock-and-roll tune, you know. It's gotta be a real song about real relations, or otherwise it just sounds like a songwriter writing a tune for Tin Pan Alley. I can't do that anymore. (1970)

Fogerty's reputation as a songwriter developed rapidly. "Proud Mary" was covered by a host of artists, including Solomon Burke, Sonny Charles and the Checkmates, Elvis Presley, and Ike and Tina Turner, whose 1971 version sold over a million copies.

John Fogerty

I like [soul singer] Al Wilson's recording of "Lodi." And it's funny because he doesn't read the song well. He doesn't know what the song is about. He doesn't do it well, but I like it, for a record, you know. Completely separate from us, as if somebody else had written it. It was quite a shock to hear that, because the band really cooked. I thought, "Whoa, it's like a brand new song!" He doesn't sing it as if he knew what "Lodi" is about. He makes it sort of happy, at the very worst just a *little* melancholy, you know. But not sad, not a downer at all. But I liked the record and the melody fit and everything.

Solomon Burke picked up what "Proud Mary" was about. I loved his version more than any other. He knew what it was all about, really. It's an escape song. He blew a few of the heaviest lines in the song. He probably didn't understand the way

The songwriter in the Fantasy stockroom, 1969
(Courtesy Graham Niven)

I sang the words. But he tells you where he's at in the beginning of the record. Tina Turner's version of the same song is really far out—especially when she does it in person. She and Ike really rip it up.

The Hollies's "Long Cool Woman" was Creedence's greatest record! It's the way I feel about Gene Vincent's "Be-Bop-A-Lula"—that was Elvis's greatest record! . . . Just the *vibe* coming from "Green River" and a little bit of "Bad Moon" and just kind of going off into the Creedence repertoire. And that's okay; unless you're actually stealing the song itself, the sound and the arrangement are just there for the asking, really. (1969, 1970, 1997)

Over the years, Fogerty has often reflected on the origins and significance of specific songs. The stories behind "Proud Mary," "Lodi," "Fortunate Son," and "Run Through the Jungle" can be found in Chapters Three and Four. What follows is a compilation of some of his most interesting reflections on some of his other songs.

John Fogerty

"Bad Moon Rising":

I've literally been trying to write "Bad Moon Rising" since 1957. It started then when I learned my first chord on guitar. It's part of that one-chord dream I had. I'm still working on that hundred-guitar thing, by the way. "Bad Moon" is parallel in the rhythm guitar sound. It took about ten years to get a valid melody for it. I had just written "Lodi" and one day I had about a half hour spare time, so I sat down and got a line or two. One thing led to another and it was finished in a half hour. I had another song called "Bad Moon Rising," but it was real corny and it had different chords. I threw the song away, but kept the title.

I might have gotten the idea from all those horror movies but more like real-life things. I got the imagery from an old movie called *The Devil and Daniel Webster*. Basically, Daniel Webster makes a deal with Mr. Scratch, the Devil. It was supposed to be apocryphal. At one point in the movie, there was a huge hurricane. Everybody's crops and houses are destroyed. Boom. Right next door is the guy's field who made the deal with the Devil, and his corn is still straight up, six feet. That image was in my mind. I went, "Holy mackerel." My song wasn't about Mr. Scratch, and it wasn't about the deal. It was about the apocalypse that was going to be visited upon us. It wasn't until the band was learning the song that I realized the dichotomy. Here you've got this song with all these hurricanes and blowing and raging ruin and all that, but it's "I see a bad moon rising." It's a happy-sounding tune, right? It didn't bother me at the time.

There is social commentary in it, I guess, but I don't make a thing out of it. I'm enjoying having simple words that mean nothing. (1970, 1997)

"Green River":

I knew the next single shouldn't be "Proud Mary" again, although a lot of people would do it that way. I hated that. I thought, no, it can't be "Suzie Q" again either. You begin to create a sequence and you're looking on down the road. By the time I wrote "Green River" that was a song I'd been thinking about for fourteen years and now was the time. "Green River" is obviously a tip of the hat to the Sun Records sound, but I can't think of any real specific song. Actually, with the loping beat of the acoustic guitar and then the bass kind of doing that rocking beat on the one and the four, I tend to think of something like "Dream Baby" by Roy Orbison. Yet "Green River" was much more rocking than that song, but the rhythm treatment fit. Obviously I'm trying to sound *that* way as opposed to James Brown. One of the reasons Creedence records sound so good is that the power comes from the simplicity. Something like "Green River" is easy to play, but it's the *right* easy thing out of all the possible parts.

I'd never been anyplace. We went to Montana once. But when I was young, we used to do a lot of vacationing or whatever up near Sacramento. There's a town called Winters. And there is a Cody's Camp there. And we went there, like, every year, and it was tremendous. It was exactly what "Green River" was all about. It was like the West Coast version of the Bayous. And that part fit together. In other words, I always thought what I had lived must have been the same thing. Because, like, it had sort of a swampy kind of a deal. And there were lots of bullfrogs and the whole thing. So in that respect, I *did* live it. Lot of happy memories there. I learned how to swim there. There was a rope hanging from the tree. Certainly dragonflies, bullfrogs. There was a little cabin we would stay in owned by a descendant of Buffalo Bill Cody. That's the reference in the song to Cody Junior. The actual specific reference, "Green River," I got from a soda-pop syrup label. You used to be able to go up into a soda fountain, and they had these bottles of flavored syrup. My flavor was called Green River. It was green, lime-flavored, and they would empty some out over some ice and pour some of that soda water on it, and you had yourself a Green River. (1970, 1993, 1997)

"Commotion":

"Commotion" is something new as far as recording goes. It has a thirties big-band up-tempo style. But we don't have horns or anything. It's very fast, like [Benny Goodman's] "Sing, Sing, Sing." That would be one of the influences, but there are country-and-western records like that too. Jim Kweskin does stuff like it. Sounds like a train. It's about the drag of the city—a two-minute impression of New York City. (1970)

"Sinister Purpose":

"Sinister Purpose" is very stereo-oriented. It's a bit somber-feeling and serious but not at all intellectual. I don't take it seriously, although it has a serious subject. A Black Mass-type theme—worshiping the devil. (1970)

"Tombstone Shadow":

"Tombstone Shadow" is about an experience I had with a fortune-teller. It was funny at the time, but all the stuff she told me was true. It feels weird when I think about it. I wonder how far can I carry all this. You know, fortune-tellers pump you first and then they throw what you told them back at you. It's a blues tune with triple lead guitar and a driving rhythm section. (1970)

"Wrote a Song for Everyone":

The record Creedence made out of "Wrote a Song for Everyone" I'd say was just sort of average. I wish it had been a great, great record, because I really like that song, I think it's a great song.

That song came about when my first wife was upset with me for sitting there and writing music all the time. It was early 1969 and I was the one that single-handedly was gonna make this little airplane fly, meaning our career. The people at the label didn't know and the people in the group didn't know. It was up to John, in other words. So I was pretty busy trying to write songs and chart our course. And my wife, very understandably, said, "I'm going to take our child who you're ignoring and I'm going over to Mom's house." And she went out the door. She didn't yell at me, she just said it matter-of-fact. What I did immediately was I looked at my empty page and I wrote the words, "I wrote a song for everyone, but I couldn't even talk to you." At first it was personal, but then I started thinking about all the situations that it must be true in, like a politician who's popular with the whole country yet he can't even manage his own life, let alone his eighteen-year-old son who's having a rough time at college. It seemed to apply to all kinds of situations. Basically, I was being given life's lesson, but the songwriter in me turned it into something I could write about. (1998)

"It Came Out of the Sky":

A lot of the fun of rock is trying to figure out what he said. It's too serious not to be taken humorously. (1970)

"Don't Look Now":

Why does that matter? That's exactly why I wrote the song. We're all so ethnic now, with our long hair and shit. But when it comes to doing the real crap that civilization needs to keep it going . . . who's going to be the garbage collector? None of us will. Most of us will say, "That's beneath me, I ain't gonna do that job." (1970)

"Who'll Stop the Rain":

I wrote that in the midst of the Vietnam era. It was kind of a fatalistic view. I was a person who felt powerless. I realized a split in me: I'd grown up as an American, and I was proud to be an American, yet I realized these people in Washington weren't my country; they were representatives of the government. And with a great sense of powerlessness, I was asking questions I had no answer to, meaning, why does this have to be this way? Why are these people in charge, and yet they don't seem to be listening to us, the people they say they are representing?

I wrote that on my electric guitar, but unplugged so it sounded very acoustical. Remember, I'm a guy in a little two-room apartment, and can't be rocking out because my neighbors would let me know about it. So I would do that late at night, and it would have a very acoustical sound, so

I could imagine an acoustical sound for the song. Which means we're talking kind of folk-rock, if you're going to hyphenate what it was in those days. And you just start imagining what will work. Let's take a bass part: You don't want it to be doing what a Jimi Hendrix part would do or a James Brown part. You can't do that. You need something that complements that "do-da-chinga-chinga-chinga" of the guitar; you almost end up doing it with your mouth. And the same with the drums; It has to lock together, and it has to complement the acoustic strumming part. It can't be any more complicated or you're going to start getting into some new fusion of some kind. (1997)

"I Heard It Through the Grapevine":

I go off for eleven minutes basically in the same position on the guitar . . . there's times now when, although I don't actually sit down and play those things, I'll be in the car, just driving along, and hear them. This actually happened about ten years ago with that song; I was on the highway and four, then five minutes pass and I'm thinking, "Come on, John, do something different now." And then there was *another* chorus. (1997)

"Someday Never Comes":

Every parent tells their child, "someday." Kids grow up hearing that phrase all the time—"yeah, someday you'll understand." "Daddy, can we go fishin'?" "Yeah, someday." Certainly my parents divorced when I was young, and I ended up divorcing from my first wife when my kids were young—we separated around that time, we got back together, and finally we did divorce, which is a very sad thing. The song is basically me talking about here it happened to me when I was young and here I go doing the same damn thing. It's sad, it's unfortunate, and it's not the way kids would like it to be. It seems you're always hearing, someday, someday, someday, and I wanted to express what a kid feels, someday never comes. I wish we had played the music a little stronger on that. I wish I had really gotten what I wanted. If it was *Cosmo's Factory*, I would've. (1997)

"Centerfield":

It was my way of stating that I was going to be back in showbiz, but I used the metaphor of baseball. To me, as a kid, the greatest place you could be in baseball was playing center field in Yankee Stadium. I always had that as a metaphor in my own heart at least. One day, I put those two things together. (1997)

"The Old Man Down the Road":

All the guitars got laid on after the rhythm was there. I think I already had a rough vocal, so I knew where they would fit together. But that was kind of an intense thing, because it was all on feel. It was worked out, but I tried to make it as spontaneous as possible. The whole point was to make it as loose as I could. The guitar on "Old Man" and "Searchlight," you couldn't get a studio guy to play like that. I knew the feeling I wanted, but I didn't know what my hands would do the day we went to overdub the little parts. I have cassette after cassette with these little riffs on them. Then I'll listen to them when I'm driving around, and eventually some of them are strong enough that I want to write a song. That's exactly what "Old Man" was. To me, that's the most obvious way to make a rock-and-roll record. (1985)

"I Saw it on TV":

In some songs you just have an idea that you're trying to express. A perfect example is "I Saw It on TV." I wanted to address the fact that our age has grown up in front of the tube. How has that affected us? It was the first song I really finished in years, and it was the hardest one. (1985)

"Swamp River Days":

When I was growing up in northern California, my family used to rent a cabin near a place called Putah Creek from a guy named Cody, who claimed to be a direct descendant of Buffalo Bill Cody. My brothers and I would play for hours at a rope swing over that creek, which was also where I had a blazing-hot summer romance with Susie when we were both four years old. In this song I revisited that place, but now I'm a teenager instead of a little kid . . . someone who can drive a pickup truck down to the river and remember the same things that I remember about that place, growing up. It's kind of a mythical state of mind. When I won the "Old Man" case I said the next record was going to sound exactly like a Creedence record. So yeah, it sounds like "Green River." It's an *exact copy*. Take me to court. (1997)

"Southern Streamline":

I think it's really a picker's song, and picking makes me feel good. It's also got little dashes of rock-and-roll country guitar, but it's the steel that gives it the western swing attitude. All I did was hit a couple of those licks and the whole tune just fell into place. Pedal steel gives you what sounds to me like a freight train going down the track, or what Hank Williams once called, "the silence of a falling star." (1997)

"A Hundred and Ten in the Shade":

That particular song you could say was a direct blessing from my trips in Mississippi, because it came to me as a song. It was probably a year after my last trip to Mississippi. It was in June 1992 that I started recording. I was sitting by a dirt road in southern California out in the country trying to get inspired, when this song just sort of all arrived. I call it a gift because it wasn't like this agonizing, backbreaking stuff you do with a lot of songs. This just sort of landed with a feeling and the sound and every-thing and that's a direct visitation, a memory, from my own trips to Mississippi. The heat and the humidity and the feelings and I knew what it should sound like, too. There are things you can't really verbalize, the words get in the way. Your ears either tell you it's true or it's not true, it's right or it's not right. I really like that track. I really like that song. I was also privileged to have [gospel quartet] The Fairfield Four sing backup for me. I wanted to capture a sound that was as old as dirt, and they knew exactly what I was going for. After all, they've been making records for a very long time. (1997)

"Joy of My Life":

It's the only love song I've done. My wife, Julie, is a very wonderful and positive person. A friend of mine noticed many years ago that every time they asked about Julie, I'd always start by saying, "Well, she's the joy of my life." One day in 1990 or '91, this person said, "John, you need to write a song for Julie and call it, 'The Joy of My Life.'"

I knew, knowing my history, how difficult this project was going to be. So I worked on it and worked on it for like six years, getting it right. Getting it to where I'm speaking in plain language, the kind of language I use talking to Julie. It had to be beautiful but not overbearing, not a pompous Olympian theme. It had to be simple. After a lot of careful work, I feel I accomplished what I was trying to do. And it's my favorite song to sing in concert.

Julie's opened my eyes to a lot of things. For a while there it seemed like I was living in this cave, and every time I thought I'd run away from the lawyers, I'd get sucked back in. But I'm out for good now. The song's about as personal as I've ever gotten in my music and it's really the first love song I've ever attempted. Julie has taught me a lot about expressing myself, and this song is a little like my term paper. You know, first you take the course, then you do a rough draft, and you keep polishing it until you turn it in, and it gets graded. (1997)

"Rambunctious Boy":

There's a song on *Blue Moon Swamp* called "Rambunctious Boy" and I had an arrangement prior to the one that's on the record. It was bothering me, and I was saying, "Why is this bugging me?" But it was just too country, it wasn't honest. And I finally said, "I love Buck Owens and I think everybody knows that," I name Buck Owens in "Lookin' out My Back Door," but I'm not Buck Owens. He does what he does. That's his job. I shouldn't imitate it or try to be Buck Owens. That's me not doing my job. Let's face it, as much as I'd love to be, I'm not Merle Haggard or Garth Brooks. So I went back and started over again, until I finally came up with a Buddy Holly, Bobby Fuller Four, Texas kinda feel . . . a rock-and-roll version of country. So I changed the arrangement and made it more like a rock-and-roll approach. When I finally did that I was much happier. It's nothing against Buck. I love his music, but I shouldn't try to clone myself into somebody else. (1997)

"Blue Moon Nights":

There was a magic time in early rock and roll when Sun Records was at its zenith and Elvis and Carl Perkins and all the rest were making such great music. I just imagined some other rockabilly guy walking in the door of the studio with a satchel full of songs and having Sam Phillips say, "Why don't you show me what you've got." And one of the tunes that kid would play would be this one. (1997)

"Premonition":

One day I was out jogging and listening to the radio and this guy started talking about some topic out of the blue, and I said to myself, "I was just thinking about that." Then I tried to remember the word that describes when that happens: "Déjà vu? No. Clairvoyant? Damn! Wait . . . it's pre-monition." And I though "Hey, that's pretty cool," so when I came home, still all dripping and sweaty, I wrote the word on a Post-It note before I forgot and stuck it on my desk. And it just sat there. Meanwhile, I had about a month window to write my new song [for the album that became *Premonition*] and the time kept getting shorter and shorter, what with one thing and another. Time was running out and I still didn't have anything. Then I got my hook into one with about six days to go before rehearsals started. It had a really great riff and everything, but it just wasn't coming together as a song. Finally, with one day left, I realized it wasn't working and that I'd have to start over. That's when I remembered that Post-It note. I mean, I hadn't even thought about that in all that time, and then suddenly I had a premonition about "Premonition." I literally had one morning left and, boom, it just came out. That's usually how it works for me; fiddling around with titles and going places that end up being dead ends and suddenly making a left turn at just the right time and having it all kind of lay right out. (1998)

DEPARTURES 6

Reflecting that "the beginning of the end was almost before the beginning," John Fogerty summed up the last years of Creedence Clearwater Revival as a process of "evolving back into Golliwogs." John's response was clear: "I didn't want to be a Golliwog again." His version of the group's demise differs sharply from the one advanced by Stu Cook and Doug Clifford. Both then and now, Fogerty attributed the obvious decline of quality on Pendulum and Mardi Gras to the other members' demands for increased creative involvement. During 1971 and 1972, John attempted—if somewhat halfheartedly—to put a positive spin on the changes as part of an inevitable, if somewhat difficult, process of growth. More recently, he has presented a harsher version of the same story, one that calls into question both the personal loyalties and musical abilities of his former bandmates.

Cook and Clifford paint a different picture. The real issue, they insist, was never Fogerty's musical centrality. It's true that Tom Fogerty decided to leave the group primarily because he wanted greater freedom to develop his own musical voice. Although Cook and Clifford certainly shared Tom's desire for exploring their own potential as composers and singers, the real problem, they say, was that John demanded control over every aspect of the band's career, from song-

writing and sound production to bookings, advertising, and finances. From Cook's perspective, the musical problems on Mardi Gras—*which critic Jon Landau dismissed in a* Rolling Stone *review as the "worst album I have ever heard from a major rock band"—resulted not from the band's demand for center stage but from Fogerty's refusal to provide anything but the most perfunctory support on the songs produced by the other band members.*

The only unambiguous thing about the last year and a half of CCR's career is that the group had lost the magic that made it so central to the musical scene from 1968 through 1970. Pendulum *certainly had its high points, especially Fogerty's "Long As I Can See the Light," "Lookin' out My Back Door," and "Have You Ever Seen the Rain?," in effect Fogerty's elegy for the vision he felt slipping away. And* Mardi Gras *included "Someday Never Comes," Fogerty's searching meditation on the ways parents perpetuate the cycles of pain and alienation they experienced in their own childhoods. But it's hard not to conclude that the magic was inseparable from the group's sense of community.*

The first unmistakable sign that the myth, and the group, was in trouble came in February 1971, when Tom Fogerty announced he was leaving the band less than a month after the release of Pendulum. *At the time, Tom said he was leaving to spend more time with his family, but as the rapid release of his first solo album demonstrated, creative discontent played a central role in the decision. The discrepancy between statements made at the time and retrospective comments was to become a recurring pattern for all the band members.*

Tom Fogerty

I am not retiring. I'm just not going to tour. My children are eight and seven, and the twins are one, and this is the time they need a father with them, and they are my first responsibility. I intend to spend as much time with them as I can. It's really two separate things. If I could have given more time to my family and done what I wanted to do, and still stayed in the band, I would have done it.

It was sort of dawning on me that I hadn't been doing everything I should have been doing. Here I was, John's older brother, yet not really leading and taking the thing anywhere, and I was just sort of frustrated by it. John was always the most musical one, and therefore we considered him the leader, musically, and there wasn't any other kind of leader at that point. We didn't go around saying, "Well, John's the leader." It wasn't like that. The thing that we all understood together was that out of necessity one of us should do one thing; that each of us should play a part to make it work. The group was unique in that way. The egos were being suppressed in favor of whoever could do the job best. We tried to overcome all those things that bands usually break up over, and we did control that. Why I'm leaving isn't a result of those kinds of feelings. It's the result of another change. We were all talking about change and were going to contribute more; I found myself bouncing out altogether as a result of thinking that way. I couldn't even hang on to the idea of "group" anymore. (1971)

Since I left the group, it's complete madness—sheer lunacy—it's Tom Fogerty's freak-out summer in Berkeley. I'm just having myself a good time, a real good time, I suppose. You could say I hang out and drop into clubs around San Francisco and the area to gig with various musicians and bands. It's just great because I go up on stage as just another guy in the band. I've played with the Grateful Dead and also their guitarist, Jerry Garcia, and Elvin Bishop. I'm more-or-less jamming around and doing a few smaller clubs as a solo. I'm not trying to do a Lennon or a McCartney. I'm just doing the things I want to do. More or less, it's like an evening we all spent at the Rock and Roll Circus in Paris, when we got up and jammed with Edgar and Johnny Winter when I was with

Creedence. I'm just playing the kind of music I enjoy best. I usually sing an old Hank Ballard number, "Annie Had a Baby," "My Babe," "Slippin' and Slidin'," "See That My Grave Is Kept Clean," "The Night They Drove Old Dixie Down," and a song called "WPLJ." The scene over here in San Francisco is beautiful. You can play a different club each weekend, places like the Martin, the Keystone Corner, and the New Orleans House. You know, it's strange, sometimes there's only twenty-five people in the club. Then when word gets around that I'm playing, you get a capacity crowd of four hundred the next evening. Which is really something else after playing before half a million at Woodstock. (1972)

John Fogerty

Of course it's a change for us, but change is implicit in music. We have always been a tight personal group and we will remain that way. We're going to retire Tom's number. Creedence will continue as a trio. We will miss Tom in the band, but we anticipate with pleasure what we know he will bring to music on his own. (1971)

Stu Cook

There were certainly problems between the brothers. Whatever disagreements John and Tom had put aside, sibling rivalry was coming to the surface again. Doug and I used to joke that we felt like we were in a Fogerty sandwich. Caught between two brothers. They were the two slices of bread and we were the baloney in the middle getting squeezed. (1997)

Tom Fogerty

I felt the pressure of being squeezed. Creedence was together for nine years before we made it big, and sixty percent of that time I was the lead singer. I wasn't a dictator, but I was more of a leader than what I ended up to be in the eyes of our fans—just the guy who stood there and played rhythm guitar. So after we were into our sixth platinum album, I just thought maybe I could do a little singing. But John was not going to change things, so I split. (1982)

At the time the group presented Pendulum *as part of a creative evolution, but in retrospect all members agree that it marks the beginning of the end.*

Stu Cook

This album is starting to get into somewhat of a painful period in the band's evolution. (1997)

John Fogerty

It's just a totally practical thing. I'm not even in the realm of, "Is the stuff any good or not?" That's not the criterion. If somebody wants to do something bad enough, you're foolish to try and stop it after a point. And Tom, more than the other two guys, especially at that time, was more ready, or he felt like he was more ready. He'd been doing it for much longer. He's been doing it longer than me, really, one way or another—in front of people, I mean, professionally, or whatever, for money. So he really did feel thwarted and I can't blame him. I always had to say "No."

I didn't dig saying "No," but I always had to say it anyway. The only cut in the ego really was—what's the legal term? I had to acquire an arm's-length arrangement with myself. It's really a case where I had to detach from myself. (1972)

Doug Clifford

The changes began before Tom left. John said that from now on things were going to be different. He wasn't going to wear the business hat, the manager's hat, and he wanted more from us. He said we all had to write from now on. It was great, because we *wanted* to do more. Tom had something burning inside of him to see if he could do it on his own—so he split. It's cool. He's still just as close a friend as when he was in the band. He has more energy than anybody, lots of drive. I've always admired people with that kind of drive. I didn't have that kind of drive before because there was no reason to. Now there is and it's just great. It's like any kind of learning experience—it makes your whole head and body feel good. It's a challenge. The song I'm going to do may get blown off the record, but I don't care what the critics say. I'm not into that anymore. It's the same philosophy Tom had, only I'm finding my strength within the group. I can understand Tom's thing though—I don't have a brother in the group who is a genius.

It's a lot looser, a lot more realized. As a result, it gets tighter musically because everyone's so relaxed, and that's been the hardest thing for me to do. When I'm all tense and nervous, I play like I'm all tense and nervous. I'm not saying I still don't play tense and nervous, and I'm not totally relaxed all the time, but it's just more fun, and when it's more fun, it's easier. It was John's trip totally before and it just ain't that way anymore. I'm just totally digging that. I can do anything I want now, whereas before I was kind of afraid of doing anything. When you walk around for a long time with your tail between your legs, it starts to get to you subconsciously. I didn't say anything because, like I say, it was totally John's trip.

I've always wanted to sing. I know I have a good voice. I can't sing a Fogerty-type song—I sing more a folk-type song and Creedence has never done a folk-type song. Don't get me wrong, we did what we had to do to get where we wanted to be. Well, we are there now, and we all have untapped talents and it's time to plug them in. I personally want to do things with other artists. I'm writing songs now and I'm going to sing a song on the next album. I've talked to Stu about it already, and I told John, and he said, great. (1971, 1972)

John Fogerty

"Have You Ever Seen the Rain?" is really about the impending breakup of Creedence. Pressures, longings, for whatever reason it's starting to break up the band. The imagery is, you can have a bright, beautiful, sunny day, and it can be raining at the same time. The band was breaking up. It'll be sunny everywhere in the world. It will be sunny and yet there's a cloud somewhere dropping rain on you and you're getting wet and yet it's sunny. It can even be warm. Those are rare and weird occurrences. Blue skies, yet you're getting wet. And the metaphor I was using is that everything should have been blue skies, but instead we're having a rainy day. In a phrase I used to use at the time, we were snatching defeat from the jaws of victory. I was reacting: "Geez, this is all getting serious right at the time when we should be having a sunny day." (1997)

Following Tom's departure, CCR took a relatively extended break from live performance before returning to the stage and embarking on its final tour in the summer of 1971. In September, Doug Clifford collapsed following a show in Amsterdam, suffering from scarlet fever.

Stu Cook

The European trio tour was even more crazy. We took a Lear jet over there and massively partied. That's when Doug got sick, running a fever of 104, 105. What precipitated the breakdown was a massive security foul-up and people were just rushing in and we almost got trampled by people rushing into the building. This happened in Japan; we had to just bail on everything, leave our instruments, and sneak to the roof, where a car was waiting to drive us down this ramp and get us out of there. After a day or two Doug was back to normal, but he was quite sick at the time. (1998)

Doug Clifford

Yeah, I got sick, I think it was in Amsterdam. I had a 103-degree temperature and I was playing. I was hallucinating. I kinda went berserk before one of the shows and broke some glasses, and the road manager came to try to calm me down, and I told him he'd better not come any closer or it'd be the last step he took. [But] he's a friend of mine, I was sick, I was very sick. The good news is, we had two days off after that and I just went to my room and shut the door and slept for two days, broke the fever, and off we go. (1998)

Stu Cook

We never canceled a tour. There was only one show where John ever lost his voice. It was in St. Louis, and John opened his mouth to sing "Born on the Bayou" and it wasn't there. We started ad-libbing it, we did "Blues in G," we did "Blues in C," we did a couple of Sun Records things, we really couldn't do much because the Creedence catalog is pretty much at the top of the male singing range. It only happened once and that was because of being run down. That whole trio thing, there was so much pain associated with it. Life was just hell on a lot of levels. (1998)

John Fogerty

And then early 1972, we went to Australia and Japan. That was when Creedence was a trio. I'm glad to have had the experience, but within our own walls things were a lot less happy. We had made the album *Mardi Gras* and there was nowhere to go from there. (1998)

In May 1972, CCR released its final album, Mardi Gras, *the group's only disk to feature compositions and singing by anyone other than John Fogerty. When the album was released, it was greeted by near unanimous critical disapproval. Writing in* Rolling Stone, *Jon Landau specifically condemned the group's new democratic approach: "Ceding six of the new album's ten selections to drummer Doug Clifford and bassist Stu Cook may have been an invitation to artistic suicide for them, but it sure proves that John was right all along. That a musician of Fogerty's stature is backing him up is depressing; that we are forced to listen to Cook instead of Fogerty, insulting." At the time, the group explained the changes as part of its creative evolution. Today, Cook and Clifford tell a fundamentally different story of the band's final days.*

John Fogerty

Back in 1972, *Rolling Stone* called *Mardi Gras* the worst album ever made by a major rock band. And John *[sic]* agreed when he read it. You got it guys. You can't escape what you do. You're just better off being honest about it. It's not a time I like to remember at all. You might say on *Mardi*

A taste of the original Blue Ridge Rangers *(Courtesy Graham Niven)*

Gras we were evolving back to being Golliwogs. I really didn't want to be a Golliwog again, but there seemed to be no way to . . . human nature is a strange and wondrous thing. (1997)

Stu Cook

The inmates running the asylum? I've seen that in print. I think we all have different issues. They tie together in that we were all in the same band and they were bound to interact. Tom's desires and Doug's and mine all came together at a certain point in that we thought generally John had just taken on too much. The whole thing.

To my mind, I thought the business was suffering in terms of the bottom line. John's idea of touring was to fly a semi full of equipment out on the weekend and fly it back. Well, you can't make any money, you couldn't then and you can't now, touring like that. You have to go out, stop giving all the money to the airlines and air freight. You have to route your dates so you can go night-to-night, and the trucks can drive and people can get some rest, and that's how tours become profitable.

I have a master's of science in business administration from San Jose State, which had a better business school than Cal-Berkeley. We weren't making any money out of our great career. I saw money going out. We had a lousy record deal and we were flushing money down the toilet touring. For me, getting some kind of input into the band's business was way more important than anything else.

Tom wanted to get artistically back on track as a writer, as a singer. He was a good singer, actually. He'd fronted the band for years. He had a good early sixties rock-and-roll kind of voice, like Richie Valens or Bobby Freeman, who did "Do You Wanna Dance?" With all the cover tunes Creedence was doing, why couldn't we have done "La Bamba" before Los Lobos? We always thought it was particularly strange that John would never let Tom back in. Doug and I talked Tom out of leaving the band at least a half a dozen times.

But finally John agreed to allow input, which somehow got translated into democracy, but then it wasn't even a democracy. John just assumed it would be three to one and then proceeded on his merry way with that assumption. To me, democracy is everybody gets on a soapbox and the stuff that's good . . . when you're working with four people you can generally decide what's the right thing to do. It doesn't really matter whose idea it is. John just had too many things on the stove. When we were talking Tom out of leaving, John just said okay, okay, okay, and threw in the towel, I'm afraid, instead of taking it as an opportunity to give everybody a little more room and reunite, get another kind of revival going in the group. He just said, fuck it, if it can't be my game totally, then I don't want to play. Tom had known John longest, and he saw that coming, and that's why he quit anyhow. He knew John was not gonna make it fun for any of us to try and do anything different. So that's why he left even after we'd agreed to try and do it a different way. (1998)

Doug Clifford

What happened was, we were pretty much a unanimous group because at first we agreed on everything. In one of the contracts we had unanimity written in, which was really to protect ourselves from the label, 'cause we thought, if we break up, the label'll create another band called Creedence Clearwater and try to sound like us. So that went into the contract. By the later time, we needed to have a majority rule because things were way out of hand with John trying to run the business. It was hurting him, it was hurting the band, and it was all starting to come undone. Tom wanted to be more involved, so it was decided that it would be run like the old days, the Golliwog days, which was a simple majority. Then Tom leaves anyway. John was really upset about that. So when it came time for the trio album, he said, "Okay, you want democracy, here's democracy. You do a third, you do a third, and I'll do a third. I won't sing on your songs 'cause I have a unique voice. You'll have to do everything." That was his way of getting back at us for the democracy thing. I don't know what would have happened if Tom had stayed. You can't change what happened. What happened happened. It's over, done, it's history, it's in the books, and it's time to get over it. (1998)

Stu Cook

It's sad the way it went down. It didn't have to go that way. We got double-crossed. What we asked for is not what we got. There was never any intention to force our hand artistically. We just said, maybe jointly or individually, we can write a tune or two or something that passes muster.

What did we have to lose? We'd gone a little flat by *Pendulum* anyway.

It was a sad ending note. Doug and I felt screwed. For the outside world, for the people who didn't need to know about these problems, what did they care? They're not into Creedence because of who we are, they didn't know anything about us. I didn't like all the songs I played on, but I gave them a hundred and ten percent. I'm a full contributing member to the band, I do what I have to do. That's the way we'd always done it for the ten years before anybody ever heard of us. I knew no other way.

So when *Mardi Gras* came down, I'm like, God almighty, do I really want to do this? Am I just putting money in my pocket? I know it'll sell till word gets out. But it was more than that. I didn't want to let go of it, whatever it was going to turn into. I'd been doing it half my life. I figured, I'll try damn near anything to make it go. It was particularly sad we had to take the blame for it when you can make a good argument that nothing could be further from the truth.

We were going to contribute to the band in our various ways. I'm working on the business angle, Doug's in agreement with me on that. Doug wanted to try writing. We all wanted to try contributing, but we didn't expect that we were going to be at John's level as a writer. But John came in and said, "Oh, guess what?" This is in a limo ride after a gig in San Diego. "Oh, by the way, you guys are each writing a third and singing a third of the next album. You're singing your own songs, I'm not singing on your stuff because my voice is a unique instrument." I said, "John, wait a minute. That ain't Creedence. What are you talking about? Our fans don't want that, we don't want that. We never said we wanted that. Who in their right mind would want that from the band where it is now? It's different, but where is this coming from?" And he said, "You do it that way or I leave now."

Doug and I had to think about that for a while, and said to ourselves, well, goddamn it, we got a great band and who knows what can happen.

We're not gonna quit. So we had to put on the best face possible. We had to start talking like this is what we wanted. It would have been damaging to say John forced us into doing this. Then it came time to cut the record and John would play only rhythm guitar on our tunes. He actually left the studio and I had to sit here and learn how to play lead guitar for my tracks, slide guitar and piano for Doug's tunes. It's like Doug and I are in there making a third each of a solo album and John's doing the same. It was the most bizarre experience, but damn it, we weren't gonna quit. And then the record comes out, and it gets so heavily trashed, and John just sits there and lets us take it all. And then he wonders why we didn't go running to help him out in the "Old Man Down the Road" lawsuit. We're still waiting for an apology for *Mardi Gras*.

The irony of the whole thing is that when John forced so-called democracy on us he was still driving the bus, only he was in the back of the bus. We couldn't do anything without John anyhow; we never thought we could. It was a band. John was the leader. John wrote the great tunes, John sang them. That part of history hasn't gotten too distorted. (1998)

On October 16, 1972, Creedence Clearwater Revival spokesman Jake Rohrer announced that the group had decided to split up. Fogerty and Clifford offer starkly opposed interpretations of the forces that put an end to Creedence Clearwater Revival's communal dream.

Jake Rohrer

This is not a happy day. Ever since Tom split, the rumors persisted that Creedence had split up. We just quit pushing after seventy. All through sixty-nine and seventy we were building and pushing awfully hard with the recordings, the tours. . . . At the end of seventy, we were the biggest group in the world, without question. (1972)

Saul Zaentz

They've got to do what they've got to do. Otherwise, later they'll be kicking themselves in the ass for not doing what they wanted to do. I look forward to it positively. If they are happy in their work, they are going to produce better records. (1972)

Doug Clifford

Basically, what happened is, John Fogerty became a control freak and made very big mistakes. First of all, trying to manage the band. This is a guy that has never gone to college and has no business experience whatsoever. Stu Cook has a business degree from San Jose, I was a history major. Stu knew that he wasn't qualified, even though he knew a lot more about business than John did. We needed a mentor, we needed a guy like Brian Epstein or somebody like that, who was dedicated to the band, who knew what was going on so we could be musicians and do our thing, do what we did best. What happened was that John signed a songwriting contract that he did not understand. He had no experience and he thought he would get his songs back in three years. That's just not the way it works. It was a standard deal that Fantasy had.

Fantasy, in my opinion, screwed us over. We have a business relationship, it's become a good one over the years because we made it work. We're there, we're stuck, why not do business and try to make it as pleasant as possible and look out for your ass. But John didn't understand it. They had those songs forever, and basically he would've been free after three years to write songs and do whatever he wanted to do with music beyond that point. Our record deal was pretty standard, low, but, man, it was a lot better than the Motown deals and the Stax deals.

There was a time when Fantasy was going to go public, and they offered

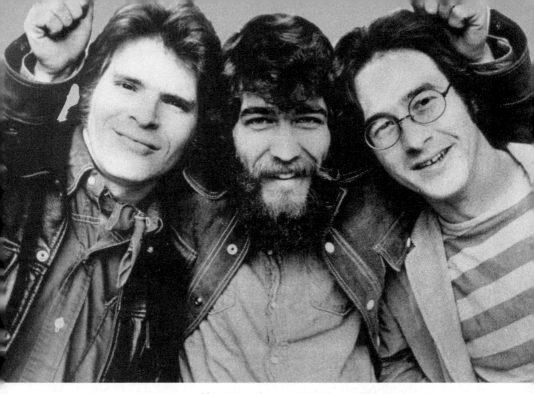

Putting on a good face: CCR as a three-piece, 1971 *(Courtesy Graham Niven)*

us ten percent of the stock, it was a stock option. Yeah, we were going to have to buy the stock, but that's the way it works with executives. That's how business is done. We were going to keep our royalties as they were and have ten percent of the company, including the films. Well, John was preoccupied with his songwriting contract, and he's going and negotiating and we're trying to renegotiate our record deal. He wanted to have his songs back. Saul said, maybe someday down the line we can work something out, but right now this is a standard deal, this is the deal we have with all our artists and that's the way it is. So John immediately got anal with Saul and that ten percent deal was left on the table for a year, and finally he'd had enough. We weren't allowed into these meetings. We couldn't get information back from John. It'd be six weeks after a meeting and you could feel the tension and, finally, we'd say, what's going on?, and he'd say, we're getting fucked, we're not gonna get a better deal, they're trying to cheat us into this stock thing and it's really a sham.

John deals with business on emotion. You don't deal from this emotional side. Business is a very cold thing. You have to take care of business. It was splitting the band up, it was preoccupying John, and meanwhile he shut Tom out from any creative participation. They used to be a songwriting team. And Tom was a good singer. We used to do a lot of covers. At least let the guy do "La Bamba." He sounded great. It was one of the better songs he did live. He sounded like Richie Valens. He went to the Del-Fi label that Valens was on with a tape we'd recorded together, trying to get a deal. John wouldn't let him do any of it. It was so wrong. Why not share that a little?

But he wanted to have control of everything and everybody and that's why it started going south. To this day John doesn't understand that. God knows, he's a great songwriter. Look what he did in a three-and-a-half-year period with Creedence Clearwater, that's Doug Clifford, Stu Cook, Tom Fogerty, and John Fogerty. All those hits came in that period when we jammed every day together, and to say that ideas for songs and parts didn't come from the rest of us is ludicrous, it's crazy.

He was so prolific when he had us. We were there straight and sober every day for rehearsal. He could count on us. We did everything we could to make him happy. We never could. We made great records. To this day the biggest mistake he ever made was to break up the band, because it was the best band he ever had. Creedence is a feel, man. It starts in the rhythm section and goes up to the great voice this guy had. It was four guys. Of course he wrote the songs and was the musical leader. But we were the best supporting cast he's ever had and ever will have in his career. (1998)

John Fogerty

I think the beginning of the end was almost before the beginning. There was a point at which we had done the first album. Everybody had listened to my advice. I don't think anybody thought too much about it. But in making the second album, *Bayou Country*, we had a real confrontation. Everybody wanted to sing, write, make up their own arrangements, whatever, right? This was after ten years of struggling. Now we had the spotlight. Andy Warhol's fifteen minutes of fame. "Suzie Q" was as big as we'd ever seen. Of course, it really wasn't that big. I looked at it like a stepping-stone. I said to the other guys, "If we blow it, the spotlight's going to move over there to the Eagles or somebody." I didn't want to go back to the car wash. I basically said, "This band is going to make the best record it can make, and that means I'm going to do things the way I want to do 'em." That sounds very egotistical, but that's what happened and the other three guys had to swallow and go, "Okay, yeah, that's what we'll do." For the next two years it worked great, and then at some point they didn't want to swallow and say, "That's nice," anymore. It was a time bomb. Here I had sort of forced my will on them because I thought it was right. Well, in terms of success, it was right. In terms of human condition, I don't know. I just really got beat down. For one thing, I was not popular in my own band. There's an old war movie where the guy says, "When you put on the clothes of the general, you cannot be popular with your men." I gave in 'cause I got tired, and that's what they wanted. Even though I thought it was wrong. (1993)

I didn't play drums, bass, or rhythm guitar on any Creedence records—not to supplant anybody else's position. We were basically a four-piece band. So each guy would do his part, and then I would add whatever else was necessary to make a record out of it. In creating this persona, I was very much a company man. In a sense, I was able to have my solo career with the band because I was doing so much. I had no inspiration whatsoever to do anything on the outside. But since the other guys were frustrated by me taking up all the space, I guess there was always a conflict—which is natural. But I never saw it that way. I thought we were doing the best for the four-piece unit and that's all I cared about. It almost seemed like a straitjacket to them. Every beat and note was accounted for—as best I could. Because I had a clearer idea about what simplicity is. And hearing a drum do something out of a calypso song right in the middle of a rock song—having about fourteen years of listening experience—I'd say, "No, don't play that there." Three or four years later, Doug would admit, "Yeah, simple is better." We always tried to make it so that less is more. But at first, it was always a struggle. Everybody would want to play too much. That was one of the manifestations of why this group collapsed. The main reason was the frustration of where we were, as compared to where we thought we should be. (1985, 1998)

7
SILENCES

As far back as John Fogerty could remember, his life rang with sound: the cacophony from the instruments his mother gave him when he was a small child; the riffs that made him a classic rock guitarist; the drawl that connected his voice with Elvis and Carl Perkins; perhaps most of all the studio expertise that shaped Creedence Clearwater Revival's greatest records. So the fact that Fogerty descended into decade-long silences not once but twice gives a clear sense of the depth of his alienation between the breakup of CCR in 1972 and his triumphant—and, he promised, lasting—return to the studio and stage a quarter century later.

In between, Fogerty's life story reads like a bizarre collaboration between Charles Dickens and Franz Kafka. Fogerty would no doubt have found it all too easy to recognize the point of Dickens's Bleak House and Kafka's The Trial, both of which chronicle the nightmarish experiences of people caught up in absurd and never-ending legal proceedings. The basic facts surrounding Fogerty's silences are clear. After CCR broke up in 1972, Fogerty released one album on Fantasy, Blue Ridge Rangers (1973). Dissatisfied with the terms of *his contract, Fogerty threatened a "silence strike." Asylum Records president David Geffen bought Fogerty's contract for a million dollars in 1974 and, in 1975, Fogerty released a solo album on Asylum,* John Fogerty *(also called the "Shep" album, after Fogerty's dog, who sits beside him on the cover). A second album scheduled for release on Asylum,* Hoodoo, *was killed shortly before its scheduled release in May 1976.*

Fogerty would not record again for almost ten years. In the interim, he grew increasingly estranged from his former bandmates, all of whom had been released from their contracts with Fantasy. The situation was exacerbated by financial disasters and the first rounds of what would prove to be protracted lawsuits and legal maneuverings. The notorious Caste Bank tax-shelter scheme, which Penny Lernoux describes in her book In Banks We Trust, *resulted in the loss of most of CCR's accumulated wealth. In March 1978, Fogerty filed suit against Burton Kanter, a Chicago attorney, Edward Arnold, an Oakland accountant, and Barrie Engel, an Oakland attorney. At the end of a lawsuit that dragged out over some five years, the former members of CCR were awarded $8.6 million in damages.*

Following the resolution of that suit, Fogerty returned to the studio and began recording the songs that were released on his 1985 Warner Brothers album, Centerfield, *which rose to the top of the album charts on the strength of the popular video of his Top Ten hit "The Old Man Down the Road." It was another song off the album, however, that was to prove central to Fogerty's immediate future. "Zanz Kant Danz" (subsequently retitled "Vanz Kant Danz") presented Fantasy's owner as a performing pig trained to steal people's money. In retaliation, Fantasy filed suit against Fogerty for "self-plagiarism," claiming that "The Old Man Down the Road" was based on "Run Through the Jungle," whose copyright Fantasy controlled. In November 1988, at the end of an absurdly convoluted trial, Fogerty was acquitted of sounding like himself. Although Fogerty released a follow-up to* Centerfield, Eye of the Zombie, *in 1986, he soon withdrew into his second decade-long silence.*

*If the events themselves can be clearly stated, their significance and the moti-
vations that shaped them remain matters of deep, and fundamentally unresolv-
able, disagreement. While Fogerty justifiably emphasizes the absurdity of
Zaentz's lawsuit, observers less caught up in the immediate conflict foresaw the
consequences of subjecting a man Stu Cook describes as a "brutal businessman" to
what Zaentz—portrayed in the claymation video as a pig—was sure to perceive
as public humiliation. Similarly, the events surrounding the "Old Man" trial
destroyed any possibility of reconciliation between Fogerty and his former bandmates. Although Cook and Clifford did not testify against Fogerty at the trial, he
was embittered by their silence throughout the litigation. Both Cook and Clifford
share Fogerty's belief that Fantasy reneged on an agreement to renegotiate a contract Cook calls "the worst in the industry." But they felt no obligation to join in
what could be seen as an attack on Fantasy, whose royalty payments were and are
their primary sources of income. Both deny encouraging Fantasy to take legal
action and maintain that Fogerty never asked for their support. In 1995, Cook
and Clifford put together a band whose live performances rely almost entirely on
the old CCR songs; the group performed under the name Creedence Clearwater
Revisited and, when Fogerty obtained an injunction, Cosmo's Factory. Although
a court decision upheld Cook and Clifford's right to the Revisited name, Fogerty
filed an appeal and the courts had issued no final decision by 1998.*

*In retrospect, Fogerty has criticized several of the choices that contributed to his
creative and personal malaise, specifically his decision to play all the instruments
on* Blue Ridge Rangers *and* John Fogerty, *and his refusal to play any CCR
songs on what he sardonically refers to as the "Zombie" tour of 1986. Clearly, the
period marked the creative nadir of Fogerty's career.*

John Fogerty

Since the end of Creedence Clearwater Revival I really went out looking
for new musicians. But I couldn't find anyone on the same wavelength as

me. So I learned one instrument after the other. Suddenly I thought my musical horizon had become endless. I could make my music the same as I heard it in my head. First the music should come across, then people could know that the group Blue Ridge Rangers consists of only one man . . . me. With my name I can't go wrong, but I have developed a new rock sound. Light, strong, but with a strong Dixie influence. (1972)

You should do stuff you're good at and favor your strengths. I've drifted into not always doing that, on some of *Eye of the Zombie* and maybe some of the cuts from *Blue Ridge Rangers.* Maybe I tried to be a little more country than I really am, so it sounded like some guy who was out of his element. I wouldn't do that album the way I did it then, with me playing all the instruments. *Blue Ridge Rangers* was a really cool idea because those songs are great songs. I love that music. It was great to not worry about writing the songs. And then just arrange it through a rock-and-roll guy's eyes. I have so much reverence for the people who really play good, like a Jerry Douglas or a James Burton, who's just a hot picker. That's something else you tend to see more in country music than in rock and roll or even in blues. The country guys are just flat-out pickers on their instrument. They're just amazing players. When rock-and-roll guys become amazing players, it's almost like they're not rock and roll anymore. They become too highfalutin. 'Cause rock-and-roll folks kind of have an attitude and a sound with some dirt in it, and blues guys are disciplined, they're regimented. You have to stay in that format. If you go outside, you can't come back in again, you're just not accepted. Will the Blue Ridge Rangers ever surface again? Yeah, with real people. I had every intention of making a record eventually with people like Jerry Douglas, who just scares me he's so great. I would like some of that on a record I do someday. (1997)

Our royalty rate at Fantasy was really low, and as time went on and we asked for that—"Okay, boss, you promised us you'd tear up that contract if we ever got a hit." It became obvious that it wasn't going to happen that way, and the frustration just got greater. One adjustment financially upward was that this lawyer from Chicago came up with a plan involving a bank in the Bahamas that would save us a lot of taxes. Our own lawyer and accountant advised us to do this plan, too.

But after the breakup of the band, I started trying to get away from that and also away from Fantasy. Their position was that I owed them all these masters, because under the conditions of the contract, if I didn't complete a certain amount in one year, they slid over into the next year, where they were joined by additional masters, and so on. I started to complain, but they were unbendable. I did the *Blue Ridge Rangers* album and then said, "I'm leaving. When I come back, we'll have a meeting to decide what to do." I told them, "Look, I can't make any more records this way. I'm having trouble just communicating with my own brain about how you put a record together." Not that these guys understood this. But the knack of knowing what a single is, or how to piece together a track, is a fragile thing. Now I know, because I lost it for ten years. I said, "The switches are going down. I can't concentrate because I owe you so much product, and it's not fair." Nobody spoke up for me, so I left and didn't go back. (1985)

David Geffen, who owned Asylum, started shopping for me. He called me right near the end of 1974, maybe early in 1975. I told him, "Listen, I'm on strike." I'd let the people at Fantasy know, "I'm never coming back here until you change some things." And they never changed any of the things, so I never went back. I basically gave them my notice, but I had to wait out the time. After the time I'd told Fantasy, "You have to fix things or I'm outta here," but I didn't have the power to be outta here. All I had was the power to say, "Look I'm never recording for you again, and if that means the rest of my life, so be it." At that point I called up David and said, "I guess the die is cast, here's the situation." He was interested in me as an artist and he worked out a deal with Fantasy. He paid them a million dollars and they relieved me of most but not all of my obligation to them. Unfortunately the million dollars went through me. I never got it but I wound up paying the taxes. Saul got the money, but I paid the taxes. That sounds like a bad country-western song. (1998)

When Geffen bought my contract, Asylum had me for what they called domestic—the United States and Canada—but Fantasy still retained me for the rest of the world for the next four albums I released. At the time I went, "Wow! That's sure better than it was. Now I can go back to work." I did the next album on Asylum to the best of my ability, but looking back I'd have to say that a lot of the switches that had gone click, click, off, remained off. The task to face yourself and be brutal certainly was off. There's a couple of good songs on there, but it's not a good record. The writing wasn't like before. (1985)

I call it the Shep album, that's my dog Shep [on the album cover]. That record wasn't a good record, and of course it was not a commercial success. I view that as a disappointment, but two songs—"Almost Saturday Night" and "Rockin' All Over the World"—are good songs. I still view those two songs as among my very best songs that I've ever written. For years and years I've thought I should go back and redo those songs one way or another because more people ought to hear them. Breathe some new life into them. That period of my life was not very happy either, so when I look back at that album, it doesn't look any better to me now than it did then.

That was it. For Asylum, I made the one album. I completed another album [Hoodoo] that I think you might call mythical. It never was released, but it was almost pregnant. It really wasn't very good; it was pretty bad. I haven't heard it since. I understand it's a lukewarm bootleg album. It's only interesting if you're a die-hard fan and you want to hear an outtake or something. [Killing the album] was a mutual decision between [Asylum's next chairman] Joe Smith and myself. Joe Smith said, "Look John, this is not a good record. We'll put it out if you really want us to, but we'd rather not. You don't have to make a record. Why don't you go home and work out whatever's blocking you?" He said this in a real kind and gentle way that I appreciated. I didn't feel humiliated.

This was a confusing and very painful time in my life. I still feel the decision not to release it was the correct one. I feel the songs and music started out with inspiration but were left unfinished and unresolved. If I had been stronger at the time, I would have worked harder to bring things up to the level that I demand. I instructed Asylum to destroy the master tapes in the eighties. (1998)

So I started working on this tax plan, trying to separate myself and to get my finances out, but the bank in the Bahamas just disappeared— gone. Practically all of Creedence's life savings were lost. The amount that wasn't lost—at least in my case—went to pay the taxes for the money that *was* lost. We sued several people involved. Fortunately, BMI, bless their hearts, didn't want to pay any money to a corporation—a cloudy entity. So those royalties piled up in an account, and never left the country. When everything came down and the castle crashed—that was the name of the bank, Castle—all I had left was the BMI money, which went to pay the taxes on the other money. It occurred to me that my next three records would be on Asylum in the United States and Canada, but for the rest of the world they'd be on Fantasy. I decided that I had to get away, so I got my lawyer and said, "I just cannot record for Fantasy anymore." So I forgave all my future artist royalties after a certain date in 1980. I no longer get paid for Creedence records as an artist; I get paid only for the songs, as a composer. I was getting such a low rate that giving up artist royalties was not that big a deal to me. It was like cutting off your leg to save the rest of your body. It was a tough decision, but my advice to any-body is to be sure you hang on to your songs. If you can, publish them yourself. Any lawyer can show you how to be your own publisher. It's very important because that's the part that lives. (1985, 1993)

I'd signed the contract when I was twenty-two. Back then Fantasy and us were in the same boat. There was no money; this was all just a pipe dream. In those days, you're thinking, "I want to get signed." You don't care if it says you owe them *a hundred* albums. It was so different from the way it is now, where you have athletes negotiating contracts. There was no precedent. You have to remember that the label did not exist then as it exists now. We were not walking into a fancy chrome building; we're talking about a lean-to. And I'm the guy who had the ideas, who wrote all the songs and arranged them and sang them. They didn't know any-thing then about making hit records, about pop radio. If we had gone to some major label who spent millions of dollars making us big stars, I could understand it. But Creedence didn't have a great career because some guru oversaw us and groomed us. Creedence was self-contained. We did all the work. The worst part is the way they tried to hang on till death do us part. Everybody else in the band got released back in 1973. But they had a death grip on my ankle. (1985)

While John Fogerty was struggling to maintain his musical voice, his broth-er was immersing himself in the Bay Area music scene, where he established a reputation as a talented instrumentalist and producer. Tom recorded nine solo albums (some released under the name of his group, Ruby) and made several recordings with Bay Area musicians, including Merl Saunders and Jerry Garcia, before his death from respiratory failure associated with AIDS (which he had contracted during a medical procedure) in 1990. His collaborations with Saunders on Heavy Turbulence *and* Fire Up *are probably the best post-Creedence music created by anyone other than John Fogerty.*

Tom Fogerty

I've been living with bits and pieces all these years, but I've never gotten it all together and recorded it, at least not at the level of competency I've reached as a musician. When I used to write songs it was at a point where I really couldn't have thought about arranging because I really didn't know enough about the musical part of it. I've reached that stage now, and I feel like I owe it to myself to complete it. [I'll be making] rock-and-roll music. That's where it always was. That's the only kind of music I know. Now I can look back at it all and I can truthfully say that I'm absolutely sure that I made the right decision to quit Creedence when I did. It was all too frustrating for me to take any longer that there just wasn't any room in the group. I didn't realize this until the very end, that I was working under those conditions. At the time I couldn't see it because the group was so busy and doing so well. Now I'm on my own and I feel so much better. My playing and my whole attitude towards everything is so much better. . . . It's definitely more positive. There are no hard feelings between me and the group—we see each other at least once a week when we are all home. (1971, 1972)

Merl Saunders

We were together for about five years. We also did some early video on Tom. It was rock-and-roll video before they had video on television. It was in color and everything. I keep asking the engineer for it. I think it was called "Media Man." It was done right there in the Fantasy studios to promote the album and I don't know whatever happened to it. That was the first MTV; MTV wasn't even started then. (1998)

A break from the silence. John Fogerty jamming with Jerry Garcia of the Grateful Dead. Oakland AIDS benefit, 1989.
(Courtesy Graham Niven)

Tom Fogerty

Apart from doing the vocal, I also played lead and rhythm guitar on ["Media Man"]. But at the moment I'm only recording if and when I feel like it, which may be only once a year. But I've got some plans to record a session in one of the clubs using Fantasy's sixteen-track mobile unit. That would be much nicer and much more fun than in the studio. As yet nothing has been decided, for to tell you the truth I haven't any other plans except to continue just making appearances on the local club circuit. I'm not looking any further than that and change [my plans] from day-to-day. I just enjoy the fact that people are coming along to see me and that I've got an opportunity of meeting and playing with some very down-to-earth people who aren't on any kind of personal trip. I'm doing this pure-ly for fun and not for the money. (1972)

Merl Saunders

I didn't play with Tom until we moved to Berkeley. We were in the stu-dio. I came back to San Francisco in the early seventies. Creedence had made their mark and actually had stopped playing. I stayed out of their breakup because I knew both of the brothers very well. I was always try-ing to tell them, "Why don't you get back?" They just kind of dummied up, both of them. They did get back when Tom got married. John start-ed getting out there. Tom was a very sweet guy. John became a person I didn't know.

Around the time Creedence broke up, I went into the Fantasy studios and they wanted me to start recording again. I had never actually left them or anything, I was still up on the contract. So I had the idea for this gospel album. I went to Tom and said we have to convince Saul Zaentz to record this album, 'cause it's gonna be big-time. Gospel has never been played this way. Tom heard it and he believed in it so we went to Saul Zaentz and he gave us a budget and we started doing things together. When I started playing with Jerry [Garcia] I said come hang out with us, man, play some guitar. He wasn't doing anything and that's how we started our close relationship. We did the first record on Walter Hawkins, who, years later with Tremaine Hawkins, became, like, really big. I think the name of the group was Walter Hawkins and Selah. We had Edwin Hawkins on it too. It didn't do anything then. They rereleased it eight years later and it started selling. And it was all history about the Hawkins family. What these guys are doing now, the Winans, the Hawkinses were doing that twenty years ago. They were doing that thing, you don't say Jesus, you say baby, same music. They didn't say Jesus, I love you. Tom was really into that.

He was a very marvelous person, a very good musician, he had a heck of an ear, a great sense of rhythm for backing up. He was not heard, he was felt. John was the creator, you can't take that away from him, history tells it. But Tom was a very good rhythm guitar player. Tom was a very, very sincere guy with his music. He helped me out quite a bit, producing the *Live at Keystone* albums. He wasn't just physically there, he'd call me up at two o'clock in the morning: "You still there, Merl? Get your ass down here. I know you got everything under control." Come in the next day, he'd listen to every part. Then he'd make some comments, and if he didn't like it he'd say, "I can do my part better." So he'd run in there and do his part better. He was a perfectionist. He amazed me, some of the things he could do. He was not heard, he was felt, that's the only way I can put it. On my records, he was on a whole lot of them. He was on *Heavy Turbulence* seventy-one, seventy-two, seventy-three.

He had a great sense of timing, cagey sense of rhythm. He was the backbone of Creedence as far as that rhythm's concerned. He made it click. He knew the blues, he knew rhythm, he knew the changes, he knew that feeling. For a white boy, he had it. Tom was into the blues. He sang with the Saunders-Garcia Band, he sang some outright down-home blues, the Delta blues, the real stuff. He was into the real deal. He knew it when he heard it, and he was very cool about that. John got heavy into it; you can hear it in his voice. It's raw, you know. But when they sang together, they still had that Fogerty blend, it was very unique, very good. John has gone on to other heights, but there'll never be another Creedence. It was just that high school mentality, that high school sound, that rawness, the mistakes, everything raw, that singing. You only get it with those four musicians. I'm sorry they can't get back together again, but that was Creedence, with John fronting it. (1998)

Tom Fogerty

You'd be amazed at the notoriety that still exists whenever I go somewhere. As soon as they hear my name, they associate it with Creedence. Every day of my life, someone asks me about Creedence. Fame hasn't really gone away. It's just on a little different level. I get enough recognition, and I sign enough autographs. I don't feel like I just disappeared or something. And when I'm driving down the road and I turn the radio on and there's another Creedence song, you just go, "Yeah!" (1987)

In the meantime, Clifford and Cook pursued their own projects, beginning with Clifford's solo album, Cosmo, *which was released in 1972. During the seventies and eighties, they produced and played for a variety of groups, including the Don Harrison Band, Southern Pacific, and the Sir Douglas Quintet. During the late nineties, Cook and Clifford put together Creedence Clearwater Revisited, which performed the group's classic songs and released a double CD, aptly titled* Recollection, *in 1998. In yet another chapter of the legal story, John Fogerty brought suit against his former bandmates, who then began performing under the name Cosmo's Factory until a court ruling upheld their right to Creedence Clearwater Revisited. Fogerty appealed the decision and as of summer 1998, as both Fogerty and Creedence Clearwater Revisited embarked on tours, no final determination had been reached.*

Doug Clifford

I made [the solo album] because I owed Fantasy four records according to our contract. Stu and I had a plan. We had a lease on the building and there was no remote recording vehicle in the Bay Area; it all came out of

On the road again: Creedence Clearwater Revisited, 1998 *(Courtesty Graham Niven)*

LA. We thought this'd be a great thing to do. I thought, I can kill two birds with one stone. I'll bring the remote vehicle up here, drive it into the Factory, and use the Factory as a studio, and if that works, we'll buy a truck, we'll make money to support what we're doing by doing the live recordings, and we'll have our pet projects and we'll have the truck here and we'll use that as our in-house studio. (1998)

Stu Cook

Doug did his solo album out of boredom; he just wanted to do a project. He put together a great band. I could only play acoustic guitar in that band, which I did. Duck Dunn played bass, John McPhee played slide and lead. John Sebastian played some harmonica and autoharp. I thought that was a hell of an album. I was in Europe on vacation when he was doing it, bumming around on my motorcycle. I'd talk to him on the phone, and he'd say, "I almost got my album done," and I said, "Hey, save some for me."

It was recorded at Cosmo's Factory with a remote truck, and that's where Doug and I got our idea to start our production company, Factory Productions. We drove the remote truck and kept it parked inside the Factory. We did recordings in there in Creedence's old rehearsal area, and then we'd unplug it and take it out. We recorded Walter Hawkins; we did the Concord Jazz Festival. We made that our career for a while. But Cosmo's album was the seminal thing.

We signed Don Harrison to our production company in 1974 or 1975, it was DS&R at the time, Doug, Stu and Russ Gary. Don was an artist Russ knew from Los Angeles, he had a real rock-and-roll voice. The first album had a cover of Merle Travis's "Sixteen Tons." We had a great arrangement of that. It was a big radio hit, but Atlantic never sold much product. We did another one called *Red Hot*. Doug and I call that one *Red*

Cold and Ready to Fold. We started having problems with Don, so that project fell apart. About that time Doug and I took a break from each other in terms of business. It wasn't till 1985 that we played again. [Meanwhile], I was just having a good time traveling and partying.

Then, in 1985, John McPhee called me and asked me if I'd be interested in playing bass in a band, Southern Pacific. It was kind of a country session project. The lead guitarist in that band was James Burton. James Burton is the king of chicken pickers. McPhee was the fiddle player and the pedal-steel player.

So those guys decided to leave and McPhee saw a guy who looked like Cosmo at a hotel pool and he thought of me—that's how we're joined at the hip. So I ended up doing three more albums until the band broke up in 1990. The record company didn't understand how to promote it—what do you do with a band that's got two Doobie Brothers and two guys from Creedence? By that time a lot of the Creedence fans and Doobie fans had left rock music and gone to country music. That was the first big rock exodus, when heavy metal popped on the scene. So they could have done something, but they did nothing. They didn't even put the first two albums out on CDs. We had some problems; we went through lead singers like revolving doors. I think we could have been more than a pioneering band. Groups like the Mavericks and country bands that're selling platinum just walked over our graves onto the charts.

McPhee, [former Doobie Brother Keith] Knudsen, and I put together a band called various things, one of them was Beat Street, and recorded an album, but our managers kept dying on us, and finally we figured, hey, maybe this just isn't gonna happen. For a while, I just played a few club gigs. I played some with a band called Bad Meat; with a singer and a harmonica player we'd play a club on Van Epp Street. Wherever I could play, I'd just hang out and play a little bit.

Then in January 1995, this lawyer, John Mason, a big-time entertainment lawyer, said, "Look, if you guys can put together anything, I might be able to get you some work." Doug and I had just two weeks before said over a beer, "Man, it'd be great to play together again." We didn't want to start at the bottom, do the club thing again. Almost simultaneously, we said, "Why don't we do what we've always done?" After the Hall of Fame, we realized, we'll never play with John again, he'll never play with us, which is the same thing. We decided, if we could put together an outfit that could do it justice, we'd then see about getting this work. Well, we put the band together and, of course, there were no gigs for months and months and months.

Finally, a friend of [Creedence Clearwater Revisited lead vocalist] John Tristao's promoted a couple of shows, and management got an agency there to see us, and they got us five more gigs, and those five got us to [booking agency] ICM, who've gotten us a couple hundred gigs. We toured Asia, we toured Korea, two shows in Seoul, three shows in Thailand, a show in Djakarta, a show in Tokyo, a sixteen-show tour of Europe in 1996. I can't believe the grief Doug and I have gotten over just wanting to play. We could have chosen another name, but we believe we have the moral right to the name. We're the guys who played them in the first place and that right gets proven by the audience every time we play a concert. We think the *Recollection* CD's representative. But we're better since we cut the album. It was recorded the last three nights of five in a row after a year of god-awful touring since we were Cosmo's Factory for most of the year, when we had to change names because of the suit. Nobody's being fooled. We've never had to refund a dime. After three or four songs, it just becomes the Creedence experience for the audience. It's really the same as when we left, the audience reaction. It feels too good to be wrong. With all the hate and pain in the world, what's wrong with a hundred minutes of fun? (1998)

The only momentary thaws in the relationship between Fogerty and his band-mates occurred in 1980 and 1983, when the band reunited briefly to perform at Tom Fogerty's second wedding and the twenty-year reunion of their class at El Cerrito High School.

Doug Clifford

The thing at the high school reunion was really odd, actually. John asked me if I wanted to play, and I was shocked that he even showed up—and even more shocked when he asked me if I wanted to play. John said, "We'll do three tunes, and the last one will be 'Proud Mary' and by the time we get up there, I'll figure out what the other two will be." An hour and ten minutes later, we did "Proud Mary." We would have liked to have played longer, but we ran out of tunes. We did "Hully Gully" and "Annie Had a Baby" and a lot of tunes that we did when we were the Blue Velvets. From the moment they announced the Blue Velvets were gonna play, everybody went nuts. (1984)

Tom Fogerty

I was hoping [after the wedding performance] there would be a lot of dis-cussion. But a couple of days went by and John was gone again. There's a bitter emotional problem that's evolved, and there're these differences that I would have thought in time would have disappeared. It's like you have fights with people, and then you have a hurt, and then time heals. I would think it would have just dissolved by now, but it hasn't. (1982)

Although Tom had wanted the group to play together at least one more time, John remained deeply estranged from his brother and the rest of the group.

John Fogerty

Unfortunately, Tom and I never reconciled in a meaningful way. I went to see him when he was very ill in the hospital a few times, and I was the correct family brother. One of the last things Tom said to me was, "Saul Zaentz is my best friend." It's like you look at the guy and, like, wait a minute. You know all the pain I've been through. You know the contracts, the cheating, all of that stuff, how I alone have been the one who paid the price from our group that made him so enormously wealthy and successful. How can we be sitting here talking about reconciliation and you hit me with something like that? It hurt me terribly. It still hurts. Blood should be thicker than water. (1998)

In 1985, Tom Fogerty made what will probably be the last statement that treated CCR's myth of community as a possible reality. "Creedence was and is the Fogerty brothers, Doug Clifford, and Stu Cook," Tom said. "Two brothers, two friends, and a beautiful dream." But it was clear that the dream belonged to the past. After Tom's death, the surviving members of CCR made their feelings about a possible reunion absolutely clear.

John Fogerty

Too much has happened for me to consider it. (1997)

Stu Cook

Before we could ever play again we would have to talk, and talk deep and long. (1997)

Doug Clifford

I will never play with John Fogerty again. (1997)

In 1985, John Fogerty emerged from a decade away from recording with Centerfield. *The album's similarity to CCR's sound was the source both of its tremendous commercial success and of the next round of Fogerty's legal entanglements. In 1986, Fogerty toured for the first time in fourteen years. Determined not to contribute to Fantasy's economic well-being, he refused to include any old CCR songs in his mid-eighties concerts.*

John Fogerty

I had lost the sense of how to make a good record, or even write a good song. It's a long, sad waste of time when you think about it, but then I didn't really sit around and waste time. I built an office and rehearsal studio and I would get up at eight in the morning like everybody else, pack a lunch pail, and go to work. I taught myself to play drums, saxophone, bass, keyboards, and worked on my guitar chops. I figured I would create a style for a sort of mythical band, and I told myself that once that was done, I would be able to write and arrange songs again. For a lot of that time I was thwarted from doing what I wanted to do by legal and financial entanglements with Fantasy Records. During the early stages, I owed them so much product it was going to take me something like twenty years to live up to it, and then much later, after I had freed myself from that, I was still tied to them financially. You can't really be creative in that kind of situation; the ability to do it just leaves you. The lawyers and accountants helped things drag on forever. It just didn't seem to be moving forward, and I had to do something to keep from going nuts. My mind didn't really get free from it until last year, when a trial went in our favor; that really kind of opened me up. The songs started to flow then, and I knew I was on the way. I'd like to put together a band, but not right away. I think I should make another album first so I'll have enough songs to perform. I just couldn't play the Creedence songs. I know those songs made a lot of people happy, and I'm very proud of that body of work, glad that people continue to like it. But with what happened to me, legally and financially, as a result of it, well, it just leaves me with a kind of bitter taste. It's just that it's caused me so much pain for so many years, it's hard to contemplate playing them again. Maybe there'll come a day when I soften; I don't know. But I do know that music is not a business; music is a joy. Finally, I've discovered that part again. That's something all these businessmen have never experienced in their lives. (1985)

When I was making *Centerfield*, I finally got to a point where I had six of the tracks finished and mixed. And I was having trouble with the last three. I needed some outside input, so I brought the six that I had finished down here to Warner Brothers, which was my record company, basically because I was worried. What if they just listen and go, "John, you're stuck in the seventies and this is the eighties." I was ready for them to tell me anything, because all I was doing was doing what I know. Not only did they not say anything like that, they said, "Man, this is great, this sounds really good." I got a lot of very positive feedback, especially from [Warner Brothers president] Lenny Waronker. He had a way of patting me on the back and taking me under his wing and going, "Man, go back and finish the rest of it and let's go for it." (1997)

I feel very up about the *Centerfield* material now. I'm really glad that's there; otherwise I look like a schmuck for thirty years. There were really three songs on that album, the song "Centerfield," "Rock and Roll Girls," and "Old Man." I think I was pretty well back in my game, but I think I was still somewhat confused about who I really am. I always thought

Centerfield was a good pop album, but I thought it was kind of like a Whitman sampler. I was hitting all around but really wasn't definitive about who I am, what kind of a musician I am, what kind of a writer, what my true persona is.

The next tour was 1986 around *Centerfield* and *Eye of the Zombie*. I call it the Zombie tour because it really wasn't a high-water mark. I wasn't doing the old songs, and the reception—people who were real fans came anyway, because they like Fogerty's singing or playing. But what a weird way to have to see me. I realized later that it was not a healthy point of view.

I didn't play [the old CCR songs] because there were just so many bad feelings associated with the music and with those times and a lot of it still hadn't been resolved by 1986. Without going back into all that stuff, people behaved very badly. I'm the same guy now I was then. I have high standards and I stuck up for what I believed in. And it seemed like everybody around me was all too happy just to cash in and dilute the true meaning of the songs to make money. Everybody was trying to cash in and I didn't like that. I was sticking up for the integrity in the music. (1998)

Embroiled in the lawsuit over "The Old Man Down the Road" and "Run Through the Jungle," Fogerty recorded a follow-up to Centerfield *that studiously avoided the swamp rock sound.* Eye of the Zombie *had an explicit political emphasis rare in Fogerty's work, but failed to attract an enthusiastic audience.*

John Fogerty

Rock and roll should really be upbeat and it should have a lot of energy. Now that doesn't mean that sometimes people aren't yelling and they're angry, whatever, they want to kick out the jams. But there should always be energy. The best kind of energy is stuff that makes you feel good. I do a lot better when I'm residing there. My record *Eye of the Zombie* was decidedly in the negative direction, in the other direction. People have told me since when I say things like, "Yeah, that was a mistake, that was depressing," they'll go, "Well, maybe you had to go do that so you could get here." Maybe there's some truth to that. I didn't want to go back into that depressing negative territory anymore.

The album taught me something about politics and music. I'm a rock-and-roll guy and I'm a music maker first. I consider *Zombie* kind of an overindulgent mistake, just too much preaching, too much soapboxing. Where do I get off coming off with all that stuff? It was just too much and therefore the album became almost unlistenable. It wasn't something you'd gravitate back to. If I was lucky somebody'd buy it and maybe listen to it once. I mean, I could barely listen to it. I don't listen to it now. It has some moments, but it's not well constructed. I don't encourage anybody to buy that record. So if life indeed is a learning process then I did learn a few lessons from that record. The foremost lesson being that what I do should be entertaining. You shouldn't scare people to death or over-preach them. The kids know this from Sunday school, the rules and everything. God's gonna punish you. The kids don't wanna go back there. They'd rather play hooky or go fishing. (1997)

The "Old Man Down the Road" trial marks a high point of absurdity in the history of music and the legal system that will probably never be surpassed. Over the years a constant string of court cases have investigated the tenuous boundaries between stylistic similarity—pretty much unavoidable in a rock-and-roll format—and plagiarism. Chuck Berry won both royalties and songwriting credits in a case involving "Sweet Little Sixteen" and "Surfin' U.S.A."; George Harrison lost a case involving "My Sweet Lord" and the Chiffons' "He's So Fine"; CCR had reached on out-of-court settlement in a case involving

"Travelin' Band" and Little Richard's "Good Golly Miss Molly." But no one other than John Fogerty has ever been sued for sounding like him- or herself. By the end of the "Old Man" trial, Fogerty had been subjected to countless hours of circular questioning by Fantasy attorney Malcolm Burnstein and forced to demonstrate the nature and limitations of swamp rock by playing his guitar on the witness stand. A few excerpts from the voluminous court transcript provide a representative taste of the whole sorry mess. The "questions" in the transcript were asked by Burnstein, the "answers" were provided by Fogerty, with occasional assistance from his attorney Ken Sidle.

Have you listened to any music to prepare for this deposition?
No.
Sidle: The question was, did he listen to any music to prepare for this deposition?

Right. I assume he listens to music often. I don't want to go through his life listening to music. We would be here a very long time.
Well, we did listen to a cassette or two at my office yesterday.

What did you listen to?
Actually, these were cassettes that I have made over a period of ten years. We listened to maybe ten seconds of one of them, which was a bass-and-drum motif. That's all we listened to.

What are these cassettes that you made over this ten-year period?
You just described them exactly.

What is on them?
Basically, small portions of music, either guitar riffs or bass lines or saxophone melodies, any or all of the above ways that I prepare songs. These are musical ideas that I wanted to commit to tape so that I would then be able to recall them years later, if need be. I don't read music, so I can't write music down in that manner. So I kept my daily work or the best of my daily work on cassettes.

Can you tell me how you prepared the cassettes? Let me be a little more specific there. Would you take four—, eight—, sixteen—, whatever track tape that you were working with, that you thought had a good riff, or whatever you are talking about, and transcribe some of that onto a cassette? Is that how they were made?
Yes.

This is done over a period of years, you say?
Yes.

How many cassettes are there covering this period of time?
Maybe twenty.

Are they labeled or marked in some way?
There's no real system. Some of them say things like December eighty-two and then other ones say things like Number Three, except that I think there may be several Number Threes and several Number Fours, et cetera.

Is the one you listened to yesterday marked in some way?
I believe it was marked "Working."

"Working?"
Uh-huh.

What on that cassette did you listen to?
We listened to about ten seconds of bass- and drum-playing, something I have no recollection of, really, except that it sounded pretty good. It's not really a song or a—it's a musical idea upon which later I may be able to write a song.

Is there any part of "Run Through the Jungle" on any of those cassettes?
No.

Any part of "Old Man Down the River" on any of those cassettes — "Old Man Down the Road?" I'm confusing your songs, pardon me. I'll just stick to "Old Man." It's easier for old men like me.

I believe that portions of the process by which I finally wrote "Old Man Down the Road" are on one of these tapes or two or several of these tapes.

Do you recall what markings are on any of the tapes on which any portion of the process of "Old Man" are located?

No, I don't.

Do you have any system whereby you can locate something that you knew you put on a cassette some time ago and you thought would work well in something that you were working on at the moment?

I had no such system when I was recording those cassettes that we are speaking of. But over the last eight months, I generated another twenty or twenty-five cassettes while working at Warner Brothers writing my new album, and I took much more careful notes of what was on the new cassettes.

Do these old cassettes now — to distinguish them from the ones that come from your not-yet-released album, I assume you are talking about — do these old cassettes contain only an instrument or is there any vocal on any of them?

There may be a vocal here or there but generally speaking, ninety-nine point nine percent of it is just instrument.

Is it almost all guitar or does that go across-the-board, too?

It goes across-the-board. Sometimes it's only a guitar riff, ten seconds, and sometimes it's a complete musical idea meant to be a song.

What is a musical riff?

I'm not sure I can answer that. A short series of musical events.

Are they related in some way?

Are who related?

The musical events that you are talking about that make up the musical riff?
Well, I'm no expert, but the way I categorize a riff, it can be done on a snare drum, it can be done on a guitar, it can be played on a saxophone. It's just a series of musical events, meaning notes which have a pitch, and also a relationship in time, and usually a short idea; something that lasts ten seconds or less.

So if I understand you correctly, there is no portion of "Run Through the Jungle" on any of these cassettes?
Not that I know of.

Some of the most tortuous segments of the trial involve *"Vanz Kant Danz,"* which they refer to throughout as *"Zanz Kant Danz."*

Don't [these articles offered into evidence] indicate to you that [music critic] Robert Hilburn was saying that he and/or others believed that you were referring to Saul Zaentz when you wrote the song "Zanz Kant Danz"?
Well, the gist of the second article, Exhibit forty-two, seems to be saying that Mr. Zaentz thinks the song is about him.

Did you tell Mister Hilburn or anyone else that it wasn't about Zaentz and you regretted it if Mr. Zaentz thought so?
I didn't say anything about regret. I just told him I wrote a song about a pig.

You have been very careful to say nothing about that phrase in talking to interviewers about that song; is that correct?
I've limited conversation to that phrase, yes.

Is that because you don't want to tell them what's on your mind?
I think it's more simple to say that that is what the song is about. There's no reason to analyze it any more than that.

So if Mr. Zaentz feels that the song was written about him, and if many other people in the industry and

general public feel that the song was written about Mr. Zaentz, you would find that no cause for concern; is that correct?
Sidle: He would find it no cause for concern?
I wouldn't say that I'm not concerned.

What is the level of your concern? That you have been sued? Is that the extent of your concern?
I'm concerned about this lawsuit, yes.

Are you concerned that Mister Zaentz's reputation was damaged?
Not specifically in those terms.

How about generally?
Generally, yes.

Generally, you are concerned that Mister Zaentz's reputation was damaged?
Yes.

What have you done in talking to any reporter or interviewer to undo any such damage by saying you did not intend to refer to Mr. Zaentz in writing that song?
In those specific terms, I have not done anything. . . .

In the course of that short discussion, what was it that [Warner Brothers executive Mo] Ostin said, to which you responded, "I wrote a song about a pig"?
I can't remember precisely.

Give me your best recollection as to what he said.
It was simply—I'm sure he was aware that there was a man called Saul Zaentz and here was a song called "Zanz Kant Danz." And I replied, "I wrote a song about a pig."

Did he say something to the effect of, "Hey, isn't this going to get us into trouble?"
I can't recall it that way. I think the subject may have been sort of thrown around, and we didn't

feel — no, I shouldn't say how other people feel.

Right. . . . Did anyone at that meeting say anything at all about any of your music on that tape sounding like Creedence?
Sounding like Creedence?

Yes.
I think — let's see. What they said, not what I got out of it. I think there was some discussion between me and Lenny about the order of songs. And I wanted "Old Man" first because it was definitely the style of music to which I am very closely identified.

Is that what you said?
Not in those exact words.

Well, but is that the substance of what you said?
Yes.

Did he express any kind of disagreement with that?
No.

Did anyone say anything at all at that meeting to the effect that any of the selections on the tape that you played sounded like your old material?
Yes.

Who said that?
All three.

All three said that?
And so did I.

And they were pleased with that, weren't they?
Yes.

Were any specific titles mentioned of your old music?
I believe so.

Which ones?
"Old Man Down the Road."

I'm talking about your old music.
Oh, no.

Well, let's go back, then, to the question that you did answer. Which titles of the tape that you played were mentioned by anyone at the meeting as sounding like your old music?
When I played the record, the first song is "Old Man Down the Road." It starts with a very distinctive John Fogerty guitar riff, and then, within ten seconds of its starting, everybody sort of looked at me and smiled and said, "Boy, this sounds great."

I think the question was, what selections did they say sounded like your old stuff.
Mr. Sidle: Well, I think that question assumes facts not in evidence: that they did put it that way. We are trying to get what they said.
Mr. Rudman: He testified that they put it that way.
Mr. Burnstein: Yes, he said that already. I just want to know which selections now.
Mr. Sidle: No, no. What I'm saying is, somebody identified a selection that sounded like his old stuff. I thought we were talking about what he was playing for them in a general way. . . .

What about "Old Man"?
What about it?

Does it sound like Creedence music?

It sounds like swamp music. Basically it's got a good guitar lick that starts it. It's got a great solo. It's a great rock-and-roll record.

Why don't we take our afternoon recess?

And on and on and on. The transcript of the trial runs well over four thousand pages. Even though Fogerty's creative process was thoroughly vindicated, he emerged from the trial angry and embittered. Over a decade later, Zaentz, Fogerty, Cook, and Clifford continued to trade barbs. Clifford specifically rejects allegations that he was instrumental in Zaentz's decision to take Fogerty to court.

Doug Clifford

How about this one? I'll start at the very beginning. Here's a guy who is finally free of his nemesis. He signs with Warner Brothers with Lenny Waronker, who comes from the creative side, he's not a lawyer or an accountant, a dream come true. Lenny Waronker says, "If we do nothing else in my first year, we break John Fogerty." So now he is this focal part of the entire company, they're going to spend over a million dollars promoting him. It's a dream come true for John, he can finally go out and do his own thing.

What does he do? He puts out "Mr. Greed" and "Zanz Kant Danz." "Zanz can't dance but he'll steal your money / Watch it boy or he'll rob you blind." And the story's about this very talented young singer-song-writer, the people love him. Guess who that is, folks? Then this guy, his manager, who's this ogre, who's a pig in the clay animation video. He's a naked pig. Now you're free, John, it's all in the past, John, it's all over. Lenny said, "Those songs have to go," and John said, "If they go you get no album." John insists on them. What's he gonna do? He's gonna get sued. He's free, but he has to spite Saul Zaentz. So Saul sues him. It was shameful. He jumps right back in the old bucket of shit again and stirs it up.

So we're in there talking to Saul trying to get a better record deal. We're not having drinks and dinner, we're trying to get the deal that was promised way back when. So Saul says, "What do you think of John's record?" I said to Saul what I said to the disk jockey who played it to me for the first time over the phone. I said, "That's 'Run Through the Jungle' with different lyrics." Then, when Saul asked me I said the same thing. The last thing I figured Saul would do is sue the guy for plagiarism. But wait a minute, this is a guy you've humiliated worldwide with the songs and the videos.

John's said I actually had a meeting and brought the records in and played them. That never happened. I didn't have a copy of the record, I didn't want a copy of that record. I just said that. So anyway, Saul went in and played the two records and compared them. I'll say the same thing today: "It's 'Run Through the Jungle' with different lyrics." That's all I said. I never intended to hurt John Fogerty. I can't say the same about him. But stop and think about it. Here's two powerful guys with big egos. But Saul did say in that meeting, "If he wants to play hardball, I'll play hardball with him."

But leave me out of it, leave Stu out of it. We had nothing to do with that lawsuit. That was never something in our wildest dreams we would imagine. I swore a statement that got me locked out of the building, got me blackballed from Fantasy. I couldn't advance money from them as I had in the past. I was not allowed in the building. So I got it from both sides. Saul's pissed off at me and John's pissed off at me. God! Leave me alone, I'm just the drummer!

Deep down John knows I didn't do that and wouldn't do that. Come on. I'd like to sit down in a room and get rid of all these damn lawyers and get him to tell me this stuff to my face. I don't think he would, because he knows it's not true. We're spending hundreds of thousands of dollars and the lawyers are licking their chops. I swore a statement and denied it all. I swore under oath and helped him get his [attorney's] fees back. But I can't do anything to win with him. I'm not a vindictive person. I'd forgive him and give him a hug and tell him I love him if he'd honestly say I'm sorry and I'll never do any of this crap again. But I've been burned too many times. I'm sure he says the same thing about me.

I love the guy. I just don't like him. I'm sure he wouldn't believe that. I don't like what he's doing to me and Stu and my wife. It's so wasteful. I'd rather take all the money, give it to my favorite charity, give it to kids with AIDS. Stu and I have raised one hundred and fifty thousand dollars so far with our new band. (1998)

Stu Cook

If he thinks I'm gonna get up on the stand and testify for him without him even asking. . . . He never asked us. Fantasy asked us and we refused to get involved—unless they subpoenaed us and brought us in there as uncooperative witnesses, we weren't gonna have anything to do with it. And they saw that that wouldn't have been a good idea, to bring us in under subpoena. We never had anything to do with that lawsuit. That all came from Saul Zaentz. Here's a guy who's a very, very, very sharp businessman, a brutal businessman. He doesn't sue just because a song sounds like "Run Through the Jungle," which on first blush it does. But big deal. It wasn't my fight and I wasn't going to get into it. I wasn't gonna volunteer and John never asked. So for him to paint it like we left him drifting in the wind, that's nonsense. (1998)

Saul Zaentz

Well, John and the group he started. . . . Somehow his ego came to the fore, that he was the group . . . and so some of the other guys decided they wanted some of their songs on record, and everything else. Of course, by then he was a big star and everyone else was pouring ideas into his head. . . . He misrepresented to them something I had offered him and I sued him. And he said I only gave him enough money to buy a house. It was bad for me in a sense that what he said were outright lies. His brother, Tom, wrote letters to the papers saying what I said was right and what John Fogerty was saying was wrong. So he's been saying these things, but he's been careful recently not to say too much. (1998)

John Fogerty

Well, in Creedence I was the singer, I wrote all the original songs, and arranged all the music. Every note that we played was carefully thought out. And I did the producing and the arrangement and the mixing and swept out the studio when we were done. Everybody knows that. Yet after some time had passed, and especially what happened after *Centerfield* came out, you started getting these comments from other people that had been in Creedence Clearwater that somehow I was taking something, ripping off Creedence Clearwater. It kind of bugged me. They were so good at that propaganda, of spreading the idea of "Well, John's sounding like Creedence," that I would run into an interviewer and they'd say, "How do you feel about the fact that something or other song of yours sounds like Creedence?" I'd go "Well, wait a minute, I just did what I always do. In truth, those guys sound like me." It's the real truth of it. I showed them how to play the drums and the bass and the rhythm guitar and I arranged every song. But even I suffered under that. What a hell to go through. Wait a minute, I can't sound like myself because there's this mythical character that I invented called Creedence. And we all tend to say "Oh yeah, Creedence songs." It's a cartoon that I invented. And basically, it became a recording entity well before it became an in-person entity.

Finally we became a whole. Now there were four people who were Creedence Clearwater. But it took a while. So I kind of struggled under that whole thing.

And then of course the lawsuit was the same tack. It was suing me for sounding like myself. Think about it. It's the only time in popular music this ever was allowed to happen. I heard the phrase the other day, self-plagiarism. There's a nice antiseptic phrase for you. That means I copied myself, is what they're trying to say. And of course I proved that, no, I didn't copy myself. I invented something new that really sounds a lot like me. Well, you know what, I can't help but sound like me. I sound like me. Those guys sound like me too, when they play my old songs, although I don't think it sounds *quite* like me, folks. Do you find fault with Elvis sounding like Elvis? When McCartney sounds like McCartney or Dylan sounds like Dylan? No one else ever had to go through that. But because I created this alter ego thing, this Creedence thing, it was allowed to kind of bubble under in an unspoken way, kind of like a deformed half brother in the closet or something. The trial kind of brought the ludicrousness of the whole thing out in the open and, especially when the jury saw it my way, said, jeez, that's not the deal, he shouldn't have to worry about it. When it was proven to the old record company and therefore to the old band members and to the public at large that in fact I was creating new things—because I am who I am—that sound familiarly like my old thing because it's a style, I think then, at least to my mind, it put the whole silliness of the topic to rest. (1997)

THE PILGRIM AND THE BLUES

I n 1990, John Fogerty embarked on the first of what he calls his "pilgrimages" to the Mississippi Delta. Although Fogerty had no clear goal in mind, his quest helped inspire his return to the music world he had left with a deep feeling of bitterness a decade before. At one point, he found himself standing at Robert Johnson's grave, where he experienced an epiphany concerning his own place in the world.

John Fogerty

When I visited Robert Johnson's grave I had a kind of realization. There's this guy buried there, and maybe some guy named Morris Stealum of Cheatem, Beatem & Whatever owns his songs in some big building in Manhattan. It's Robert Johnson who owns those songs; he's the spiritual owner of those songs. Muddy Waters owns his songs; Howlin' Wolf owns his songs. And someday, somebody is gonna be standing where I'm buried, and they won't know about Saul Zaentz—screw him. What they'll know is, if they thought the life's work was valuable or not. Standing among all those giants, I went, *"That's* the deal here. It's time to jump back into your own stream. Nobody talks about who owns Robert Johnson. 'Proud Mary' is spiritually mine. I will do myself." (1997)

In relation to his own creative process, that was the most important moment on Fogerty's Mississippi pilgrimage. But there were many other moments of insight during his trips south; Fogerty was finally coming to a deeper under-standing of the attraction to black music he had felt since his childhood in El Cerrito.

John Fogerty

I started having this urge to go to Mississippi. That's all I can tell you; that's all I know. It wasn't like a pill that you swallow with a glass of water. But being where these legendary artists had been, walking where they walked, provided a lot of inspiration. It's amazing to me how many great musicians came from such a small area of the country, kind of like the Holy Land. It isn't very big, but something really important happened there.

It wasn't scientific or anything like that. If a guy got a grant from a uni-versity or something he'd have to have it all laid out cause he'd have to prove what he was doing, but I actually didn't know what I was doing. I had had this feeling for more than a year before I finally went, and I just kept telling myself, "You don't know what you're doing." So I didn't go, I just kept pushing the feeling aside. But I finally decided that what was behind the feeling is that I wanted to understand more about the lineage, meaning guys like John Lee Hooker and Jimmy Reed and Muddy Waters. That was enough for me. There I was trying to straighten out who all the people were and what order they came, who was influenced by who and who knew each other, who played with each other. On that trip that's all I had to go on.

It's like anything you're fond of but you don't know a lot about. You start out making a lot of mistakes. But the best thing for me was to just go there and be there because I had time, there was no rush. Each day, I'd plan out where I was going to go. As far as I know it was the first time I'd ever been in the state of Mississippi, certainly in the Delta. The state line is actually just a few miles south of Memphis, so I might have been there by accident when I went to see Duck Dunn [of Booker T. and the MGs] and he took me somewhere. But it was the first time I knew I was in Mississippi. That's kind of strange. I'd been in Tennessee a lot. I'd been in Louisiana a lot. So Mississippi was just sort of a gap in my knowledge.

The first time I went, I was really just testing the water and I really didn't get much done. But by the time I started taking more trips, what I did was to make an itinerary each day, decide where I wanted to go and what I wanted to see. So each day I would make a little plan of what I was going to do. And of course I always ran out of time. I never did get everything accomplished each day and I never did plan ahead what city I was gonna be staying in. I just kind of played it by ear. I ended up with a lot of data. I had a lot of notebooks, a lot of pictures. I had a good camera. I took pictures of everything.

I knew Charlie Patton had stayed a lot at Dockery's Plantation. That's outside of Clarksdale. And I also knew that there were some churches with graveyards in the area and I wanted to see those too. So I'd been reading about Charlie Patton but I wasn't sure my memory was correct. But I was all excited when I found where Viola Cannon, Charlie Patton's sister, was buried. There's not a big sign on the road—CHARLIE PATTON'S

SISTER BURIED HERE! LOOK! Before, I was just sort of browsing through this sacred place, this graveyard, and there was her name. I went, "Oh my God." It's not the same name as Charlie Patton. You kind of gotta know a little bit. You just have a reverence for the lineage of things. It's a joy of discovery. It's like a new thing and all the details became an end unto themselves finally. I have to keep telling people I'm not an expert, I couldn't write a book. But I just feel a lot fuller because of those journeys.

I actually got taken to a couple of juke joints. The ones I went to were in town, they were called bars, clubs. They weren't out in the country places. I saw those, but I didn't see them at night when black people were in there. There's a mingling of the races in the South that is much more casual than, let's say, downtown Oakland. It's sad and it's happy at the same time. It's sad because of the power thing. There are many more black people in those parts of Mississippi than white people, so it's sort of sad that they're the majority but they're not in control of the power. Yet I've always felt I could walk safely anywhere I wanted to. Now maybe if I went down around over the levee where no one could see or anything, maybe that would be a bad place to go in the middle of the night. But as far as walking into an all-black club, people always treated me with great respect as a stranger, trying to make me welcome. The juke joints have names like the Mad Dog Disco. Their aspirations are to something grand, but it's painted in handwriting, it's all dripping and funky. One of them had a picture of Michael Jackson hand-painted so that the picture in the patrons' mind would be something grand, but you're looking at this thing in stark fluorescent light. The juke joints have got a flavor.

What's really exciting now is that young black kids like the music of their day, of their time. They like rap 'cause that's what's going on in black music. R & B is sort of an old-fashioned music. Blues is a relic. So what could be weirder to a young black kid than seeing some white guy playing blues. That's gotta be, like, the weirdest: "Oh, you stealing my granddaddy's music here at the mall." It's a real strange concept. It's almost beyond being black or white anymore, because it's really more a vintage thing.

My trips through Mississippi were really cool and insightful for me, almost mind-blowing in the sense that I saw stuff that was unusual. I saw this land I had such reverence for. But it's just in time that the call came to me. I didn't know why I went. I had no clue why I went. I took a lot of pictures; I seemed to be wanting to get it all down. And I preserved all this in pictures; I even got a laptop computer and made a lot of notes. I've got notebooks full of stuff. I picked up records and everything.

I was just reading this vintage guitar magazine 'cause I'm into old guitars and stuff, and here's this picture of Waylon Jennings and his guitar player, and it was taken in Lula, Mississippi, in a casino. I go, "God, what?" I've been to Lula. Lula and Robinsonville are just a little south of Memphis. They're probably the first true Delta towns, and it's a strong Robert Johnson and Charlie Patton presence and lore and history there. It's like learning about Canaan or learning about Galilee. These names, you go, yeah, he went down to Lula. So when I see this glitzy casino, wow! I haven't been back since all this happened. This friend was telling me Mississippi legalized gambling and they set it all up right on the river just south of the Tennessee line, Memphis being the connection. I guess you fly to Memphis, boom, it's like Atlantic City. I got there just in time, because if that's what I'd seen it would have been all different, like going to Vegas. So for some reason I was called and allowed to be there before all that hit.

I appreciate much more now that I'm an older guy what Muddy Waters really did do. He's every bit as seminal, as groundbreaking, as epochal, as Elvis Presley. It's funny that they're both from Mississippi. It's kind of the same journey, just some years apart. Initially they went to different parts of our culture, but they ended up in the same place. Muddy Waters basi-

cally went up the river. I used to read that on the back of albums sometimes. It was a cliché. Ralph J. Gleason's liner notes on some old album—
"The blues came up the Mississippi from New Orleans and landed in
Chicago, my my my." There'd be all these paragraphs showing off his
college education, basically. And Nat Hentoff and Leonard Feather.
You'd hear all that stuff, but it's true. It's so much more awesome to realize this guy who's barely literate comes up to Chicago and plugs in. I
mean any rock and roller can appreciate that. Wow. Then he starts getting the whole thing. He made a band. Everybody else that he knew sat
on porches playing string band stuff on their acoustic guitars. But he
organized it and plugged it in. We call it a blues band, but that was rock
and roll. It was loud.

I'm not pretending to be a bluesman. I have such reverence for that
music. I don't really want to buy a blues record by some middle-class
white guy from Iowa. I'm sorry, I have strong feelings about this. It's not
really the blues anymore. That's fine if he calls it something else, but he
shouldn't say, any more than I would, it's the blues. The blues has a def-
inite attitude about how you play, and once you start getting too citified
and becoming scientific like a college professor, then it's not rooted anymore, that's for sure. (1997)

*Fogerty's Mississippi pilgrimage reinforced the insights into his voice that had
arrived when he participated in the inaugural ceremonies at the Rock and Roll
Hall of Fame in 1986.*

John Fogerty

I've thought about this for years: Where did that [Southern] sound come
from? Because I grew up in El Cerrito, California, and there's not much
Southern about that. I finally got my answer the first night at the Rock

and Roll Hall of Fame, at the first induction ceremony in 1986. I was lucky enough to induct Buddy Holly. I stood there, and either all the people who were being honored were all there at the same time or their posters. It had the pictures of everybody all around. I looked and I looked at each one of them and I realized they were all from the South. The only one I wasn't sure about was Sam Cooke, and I later found out he's from the South too. Everybody. I knew where everybody was from. I rest my case. Rock and roll is Southern, that's why I'm southern. Because what I learned from was Southern. But I didn't even know that before. If you imitate your father and other people say, gee, you imitated your father, for you, you didn't even know you have a choice. You just do what you see. (1997)

One of the things Fogerty had done during his long layoff was learn to play the dobro, an instrument that had fascinated him since the CCR days.

John Fogerty

I was down in Nashville at the Johnny Cash show in 1969, that's where I picked this up, and Tut Taylor, who was with Johnny's band, was saying, "Well, you know, you can do *slants* and *reverse slants*," and I went, "What in the world is that?!" And he said, "You know, you don't just put the bar straight across, you can slant it this way and it covers other frets." He sounded like a rocket scientist to me. So I went home and tried it for three days, and I finally said to myself, "Never mind. This is not my job right now." So I put it away for twenty-five years, until 1992, when I was at a vintage guitar show and a guy had a dobro for sale. I asked him to play me something, and he played pretty simple, too, but I thought, "Damn, that sound is *so* great." So I bought it from him because it was reasonable, and I'm glad I did, because it's a good one.

Anyway, that's where it started. I was smitten; I was helpless. The sound kind of grabbed way down in my heart, where these things go—like seeing a pretty girl, you know? If you have any chance at all, you take the flying leap and go over and ask her a question. So that's what I did with the dobro. I started without knowing anything, but the sound grabbed me and I said, "Man, I gotta learn how to do this." And really play, rather than just working up a part for a record.

I wrote the song "One Hundred and Ten in the Shade" shortly after starting on the record. And I was sitting by a dirt road when it sort of all kind of collided and I went, "Wow, this is really good, this is really good, this is beyond me, this is above me, this is better than me." I could just hear how it ought to go. I said, "This is so good you better not screw it up." It's that same bit again. You can have a great song and then you get a lousy performance, you've got a lousy record. . . . So I didn't want to mess it up. I said, "What's that sound I'm hearing?" I thought it was bottleneck guitar. So I started practicing bottleneck guitar. While I was trying to do the other tracks and stuff and even get the band track for this song, at home I'd get up really early, four in the morning, sometimes earlier, and I did this for a year. I practiced bottleneck guitar and when I got good enough, I played it against the track we had for "One Hundred and Ten in the Shade" and went, "Wow, this wasn't the sound I was hearing in my head." It turned out it was dobro.

So I kind of had to start all over. I brought home a dobro and I did the same thing, but I became more manic about it because something resonated inside me. All I can say is I became very passionate about it. I ate, slept, breathed dobro. I've made a lot of friends simply because of my dobro connection to them. The whole lore of the instrument, which is more interesting than this story, believe me. That took three years, two years playing dobro. But I still wasn't ready yet. My chops weren't there. I'm still not gonna scare Jerry Douglas, believe me. A dobro takes a lifetime to get good at. Jerry Douglas and a couple of other guys are the king whizbangs of the world, and I'm not scaring them with my playing, but at least I got to where . . . it took me three years to get to where I could play what it was I was hearing in my head. Play like a guy who had command, not just playing the first note that occurred to him.

By that time, I had enough awareness of the possibilities, I could now orchestrate the instrument to my song in a meaningful way. I used the word arrangement several times here. That's really what we're talking about, even though I don't write music. It's every bit as structured as a big band, as Glenn Miller or Benny Goodman. It has to go a certain way and I'll know it when I hear it. That's why I had to do it myself. With a dobro I was kind of on foreign turf in the beginning. And if I just turn some guy loose, he would come in and maybe . . . oh my god, my song. And that had already been happening to me with drums, bass, and guitar. I didn't want to go through that anymore, so there it is. That's my dobro odyssey. (1997)

When Creedence Clearwater Revival was inducted into the Rock and Roll Hall of Fame in 1993, Bruce Springsteen summed up what the band had meant to his generation of rock and rollers. "They played no-frills American music for the people," Springsteen said. "In the late sixties and early seventies, they weren't the hippest band in the world—just the best." What should have been a moment of triumph for the band exploded into a stark statement of acrimony and animosity when John Fogerty refused to allow Cook and Clifford on stage for the celebratory performance of the group's hits.

Stu Cook

We thought it was just tremendous that we were inducted on the first vote, no waiting around. So as things progressed, we're talking to them about what's going on with the music, what can we expect so we can pre-pare for it. They said Robbie Robertson's the musical director, he'll get in touch with you and you guys'll work it all out, you can come into town a couple of days early to rehearse. So we don't hear anything and we're asking them and finally they say, there's been a change, there'll just be a jam, don't worry about it. I'm thinking, no rehearsals necessary, I think I can still jam on "Born on the Bayou," I still know the chords to "Proud Mary" and "Who'll Stop the Rain." Then we never heard anything more about it, so we just figured we're gonna play. We're gonna get inducted, we're gonna say thanks, and it's gonna be a grand party. This'll be one of the high points of a somewhat bleak post-Creedence career. (1998)

Doug Clifford

It was a cold, selfish, ignorant thing to do. Finally people started realiz-ing the kind of guy John Fogerty was. He wasn't this poor victim. All of the trouble John got into with Saul Zaentz or anybody else was his own doing. I mean, come on, you gotta start looking at yourself. He points the blame at everybody else, which is really not true. He conspired with the Rock and Roll Hall of Fame to make sure we didn't come down before the event to rehearse with them. I was notified when we were going in and I got a phone call from the Hall of Fame saying we're gonna call you in two weeks to tell you what the rehearsal schedule is and we'll buy your tickets for you and I said, well great. I didn't hear from them for three weeks and I called and said, what's up, and they said, well, it's different now, Robbie Robertson's handling all that, it's gonna be a loose thing, why don't you just come the day of the event, is what they told me. I said, well, I'm bringing my family, I don't want to come down the day of the event. I want to see what's going on with the rehearsals, and they said, it's just gonna be a loose jam. I said, just make sure I get the tickets for the day before, I want to get settled in, it's going to be the biggest day of my career.

They did, and we all come down, Stu lives in LA, Jeff Fogerty, Tom's son, was going to play rhythm guitar in his place, and it was a pretty special event. We figured it would be a cool way to say goodbye to Creedence, by playing together for the last time at the Hall of Fame. It's the classy thing to do. So I get down there, and the morning of the event, there's no rehearsal, so fine, it's gonna be a loose jam, cool. (1998)

Stu Cook

So Doug's checked into the hotel and he decides to go down and check the drum sets and see which one he'd like to play on. He gets down there and introduces himself to the stage manager and the guy looks at him and says, "You're not playing tonight. John Fogerty's been rehearsing with a house band for a month down in the valley." That's how we found out. So Doug calls up and says, "You better sit down, I got something to tell you," and he broke the news on me. And I said, "What the hell is [Rock and Roll Hall of Fame Foundation Director] Susan Evans doing?" Well, it turns out they'd known about it all along and they kept it secret from us as well. We saw John the night before at a predinner, and he'd said nothing about it. Susan just said, "Too bad, it is what it is."

Doug Clifford

So I go down to see what drum sets are available and they have three of them set up there and I'm looking at them. I walked in and I got this sense of, there's something wrong, like something was going on with me. Everybody who was involved with the production of it, when I'd come up to them they'd walk away. I'm thinking, what the hell is going on? So finally I got tired and I wanted to get some information. I asked this young kid, obviously a guy who didn't have a lot of responsibility, and I told him who I was and I asked what drum sets there were. He says, "Don't you know?" I say, "Don't I know what?" He says, "You're not playing. Fogerty's been rehearsing with Springsteen and Robbie Robertson and Keltner for a month."

Stu Cook

We went down to rehearsal and we saw Bruce Springsteen and he said, "John's around here somewhere." So we found John and we said, "You can't do this, this isn't right." Doug and I are talking with him and Jeff Fogerty, Tom's youngest son, comes up. He thought he was going to get to play representing his dad, he's a pretty good guitar player. So he's standing here watching this whole thing go down, and basically John just said, "You left me twisting in the wind, you didn't come help me get out of my contract with Fantasy." And we just said, "This is sick, man, I don't believe this. Whatever we've done we haven't done anything to you intentionally. This is a mean move, this is vindictive." We didn't know what to do. We had a table, we were inducted, we went up and made our speeches and thanked everybody. We didn't know what to do. It was, like, a horrible, horrible evening. (1998)

Doug Clifford

I found out the day of. It was the biggest heartbreak of my life. I went from the highest of highs. My kids never got a chance to see us play as a unit, because I only had one at that time and he was too young to go to the shows. This was gonna be a proud moment. This was gonna be a great way to say good-bye and I was absolutely crushed. So I walked back up to the lobby where my family was sitting. My wife and I had been married twenty-five years. She was with us when we were the Blue Velvets, we were high school sweethearts, she's seen it all. And she saw my face and she said, "What's wrong?" and I said, "We're going home." She said, "What, what?" I told her what happened and she said, "You can't leave, you can't go, you're being inducted and he's an asshole. Be bigger than he is, don't leave."

I said, "I gotta call Stu," and Stu rushed over and they were having a dress

John Fogerty at the '98 Grammy Awards at Radio City Music Hall in New York (*Chuck Pulin/Star File*)

rehearsal, so we went down and confronted John. And what John said was, quote, "I don't like you. You didn't help me get out of my contract twenty-five years ago." Please, y'know, come on, as if we could have done anything to get him out of his contract. He's ranting and raving and screaming at us. I came close to just decking him, but I wanted to be bigger than he was. (1998)

Stu Cook

The lights went up and there's Springsteen and Robertson and Fogerty doing "Who'll Stop the Rain" and I looked at Doug and said, "Let's get the fuck out of here." So Doug and I and our wives just got up and walked out, that's all we could do. Stupid me, still thinking there's a jam session. So I go to my hotel room and get my bass and come back down. I'm there after everybody's played. Cream played a most unbelievable set. Those guys have been in fights with each other, lawsuits, fights. Eric Clapton said, "I don't think much of this Hall of Fame stuff but this evening has brought me together with two people I really love." So there was no jam. I'm standing there with my bass, end of story. We got into this war of words in the *L.A. Times*. That night could have been some kind of scene for the Revisited thing. I think it was the realization that it was over. If we couldn't play for fifteen minutes for people who were honoring us . . . (1998)

John Fogerty

Of course, at the Rock and Roll Hall of Fame they would like to have a dramatic moment, let's call it. But it was well known to all of us that John's not interested in that. And I told the people at the Rock and Roll Hall of Fame, this is my position. I'm not gonna play with the other guys. I'm not trying to embarrass anybody. They already know I'm not going to play with them. (1998)

Doug Clifford

That night we accepted our awards. I was tempted to say, it'd be great to go out playing, but we've been forbidden to play. I didn't want to make a scene. The thing that was really cool, here's Eric Clapton, a guy who's been through much more than John. John's only gone through money; Clapton's lost a child, he was a drug addict, an alcoholic, and he stands up and is a class act. I'm dying, saying what a class act, too bad we don't have a class act in our band. And when John got up to play, we walked out in protest. I went out and got as drunk as I could. Stu and I hugged each other and started crying and started slamming beers. That is the truth, that's how it happened. Fogerty says we knew about it—how the hell did we know about it? They got together with the Hall of Fame and we found out later. We wrote to everyone involved with it and the only one that wrote back was Springsteen; he apologized and realized that it was wrong. It was a very, very cold, small petty thing to do. (1998)

Stu Cook

After the band broke up, I told John one time, "You're still in that concrete bunker of a bedroom down on Ramona Street, you haven't got out of it." (1998)

Doug Clifford

Everything is personal with John Fogerty, he takes everything personally. I've never hurt the guy intentionally, but I can't say the same about him. And more than once. The Hall of Fame is typical of the kind of punishment he'd try to put out there. Why? Come on. I love the guy. I don't like him. I love him like a brother. I have a place in my heart for the guy, but I wish he'd back off. It's really heartbreaking. (1998)

Cook and Clifford remain understandably bitter over the Hall of Fame events, which seem to have put an end to any hope of musical or personal recon-

ciliation. In fact, Fogerty's actions seem incomprehensible; even if his grievances are accepted at face value—and it seems clear the story is more complex than either side's versions acknowledge—the controversy over Cook and Clifford's exclusion undercut what should have been Fogerty's moment of ultimate triumph. It's not difficult to understand why those who remember the Hall of Fame events—which took place on center stage of the rock world—respond to Fogerty's recent claims that he has reached a new level of peace with himself with varying degrees of ironic skepticism.

Still, there is substantial evidence that Fogerty, with the support of his second wife, Julie, has begun coming to terms with the demons that kept him out of the recording studio and off the stage for so many years. When Fogerty speaks, his tones are measured but not distant. Although Cook and Clifford believe he has accepted no responsibility for his own part in his problems, Fogerty does in fact acknowledge many of the mistakes he has made over the years, especially those that contributed to his creative silence.

The best evidence of Fogerty's newfound piece of mind is the music on his 1997 album, Blue Moon Swamp. *While a few songs—"Walking in a Hurricane" and "One Hundred and Ten in the Shade"—recall the hard social edges of Fogerty's CCR classics, the center of the album lies in what Dave Marsh calls a "sermon on pastoralism." Fogerty celebrates his roots in "Swamp River Days," which he identifies as an update of "Green River," and pays tribute to his rock-and-roll roots in "Southern Streamline," "Blue Boy," and "Hot Rod Heart." If there's nothing as powerful as "Bad Moon Rising" or "Fortunate Son," every song on* Blue Moon Swamp *could have found a place on* Green River *or* Willy and the Poor Boys. *And the title cut of Fogerty's 1998 live album,* Premonition, *comes very close to matching the quality of his best earlier work.*

In blues terms—the best terms for understanding why John Fogerty is a major American musician—the most important thing about Blue Moon Swamp *and* Premonition *may simply be that they exist. As Ralph Ellison wrote, the blues are about finding the strength to keep your voice alive in the face of the most brutal experiences. Ellison's friend Albert Murray, in his book* Stomping the Blues, *elaborates on Ellison's point, writing that the blues are a way of answering "the most fundamental of all existential imperatives: affirmation, which is to say, reaffirmation and continuity in the face of adversity." If John Fogerty has yet to come to terms with the people he feels betrayed him, well . . . the blues never pretended that the world was anything other than what it is: A cauldron of tensions, cross purposes, brutal experiences. The blues are a process, not an answer. One of the greatest bluesmen ever to emerge from white America, Fogerty has found a way to reaffirm his life and his creative voice.*

John Fogerty

With *Blue Moon Swamp*, I think I finally nailed a thirty-year question. I feel like I've got it right. It's an odd concept, because I know other artists like David Bowie and Madonna are people who are forever wanting to change their persona; each time they make a record they change into something else. I've never worried about it that way. Things I did unconsciously when I was in my early twenties and being Creedence, because of all the trails I went off on for various reasons, finding, rediscovering who I am was quite a process for me. I used to literally ask that question, "What am I? What do I feel most comfortable being?" And I finally found that.

I was searching for a deeper musical place and was very purposeful about it, without quite knowing why. It's kind of like that guy in *Close Encounters of the Third Kind*, who's making a mountain out of mashed potatoes and humming a tune that's driving him crazy. Something was missing and that feeling was really all I had to go on. So I just started doing the things that I thought would help me go deeper. I toured after the release of *Eye of the Zombie*. And after that I kind of stepped back. It was during that period that I met my wife and we had a couple of kids and I kept my hand in music by producing an album for Duke Tumato, a great roadhouse band from the Midwest. But mostly, I had the feeling that I hadn't gone nearly deep enough as a musician. When I visited Mississippi, I think that was the beginning of my own awakening. It was a process that continued right up through the recording of *Blue Moon Swamp*, and the end result is that I feel as if I've landed right in the middle of where I should be. I can't be anything other than what I am, and I feel very strong and very comfortable with the musician and songwriter I've become.

When I recorded *Centerfield*, it took a long time because I did it all myself, including learning to play instruments I hadn't even picked up before then. This time around, I went about it differently, because I've always felt that the very best music comes from the interaction of live musicians. Originally I put together a four-piece lineup, but after a few weeks of playing together, I began to understand that there were limitations to that as well. So I went out on another search, looking for the best musicians for each song I wanted to record. I realized that while, for instance, one drummer might be great for a certain song, there was someone else who could get what I was after on another track. I'm playing with guys now who I always thought Creedence could be like. Kenny Aronoff is a *great* rock-and-roll drummer. I think there really is a greatness in the performance of the music on *Blue Moon Swamp* that was never achieved at any time in my career before. That's why I'm so happy. But that's what I was always complaining about with Creedence. We were very young, and the rhythm section didn't have anywhere near the tightness I thought it should have. But there's another angle you could look at it from: Our average audience was fourteen years old, and they couldn't tell the difference. They really do not hear the difference at that age.

I would just have to say from the get go it's more of a rock album because I was raised as a rock-and-roll kid. Don't get me wrong, I love to listen to the blues and country and gospel. But you have to make the choice. I just really wanted to get it right. A rock-and-roll record, a great rock-and-roll record, is more than just about the songs. It's about the playing. I would tell people during the years I was working on this, this can't just be some guy's impression of a rock-and-roll record. It has to be a rock-and-roll record. I had five or six songs right from the get go. But I wasn't getting the performance from the people. I wasn't getting that rockin' thing. A rock-and-roll record just has to have a great performance. It has to be rocking. If it's not rockin', if it's Wayne Newton, then it's not a rock record. I keep saying the same thing, but I'm trying to throw more light on it. That was really why I kept doing it. Because it wasn't rockin' and I wasn't going to expect my fans or anybody else to go for it if it wasn't rockin'. (1997, 1998)

After Fogerty released Blue Moon Swamp, *which won a Grammy for best rock album of 1997, he set out on his first tour since 1986. His performances featured both the new material and Creedence Clearwater Revival classics such as "Proud Mary," "Born on the Bayou," and "Fortunate Son." The success of the tour prompted Fogerty to release a live album,* Premonition, *that amounted to a retrospective on his career.*

John Fogerty

[The *Blue Moon Swamp* tour] is really the first tour since 1972 where I've done these songs. I have played some of them at things like the Vietnam veterans benefit and several other benefits around Los Angeles. My wife ribs me, she says, "When are you going to stop playing benefits? When are you going to play something where you actually earn money?" It's true. I've done a lot of benefits and not much of anything else. It feels great. [The tour] feels even better than the benefits because they're kind of quirky. It's a little strange to come out. You prepare for just one night for about a month and then it's all over. Whereas now, I'm sort of reassuring my fans that this is a part of me now. It's an ongoing thing.

I'm not going to, like, go run and hide under a rock anymore. It's all really connected. The only reason I'm not going to hide under a rock is that I feel a lot better about myself. The things Saul Zaentz has done or even the other guys from Creedence, mostly what they've done is lack of support. Abandonment is a pretty strong word in that situation. A lot of the things that have hurt me personally or even in a professional way caused a lot of diversions. I have to go this way, I have to go that way. With the help of my wife I've gotten past worrying about that too much anymore. They are the way they are. And things I'm sure will continue because it's their nature. But me being me is more important. It's more positive. It's a much more valuable or worthy goal, at least for me personally. I should be writing songs, making music, singing in front of people. That's my real job in life rather than defending myself.

Making good music is kind of what I was born to do. So it's also that I'm so doggone particular about the music. I mean anybody who spends that long on a record is pretty serious about it. I didn't just walk out one day and say, "Hey, I'm gonna go play the old songs. That'll put me back with the in crowd, that'll save my career." I've never felt that way about it, even though they are my songs and I had a lot more than just writing them to do with making the music. It wasn't honest to me until I could make it all one life again, which I think is what I've done now. I needed to make a record now that felt the same way as my old records. *Blue Moon Swamp* feels the same. It doesn't feel like I've gone to some weird place and gotten brainwashed by a cult. That's why I feel good about the old songs. I feel honest about it.

I knew from the beginning that whenever I got back out on the road, I'd be doing the old songs. I mean "Born on the Bayou" and the others were always a ball to play live. I've kept the old arrangements because I was always happy and proud of them, and while there's room to mess around with stuff and throw some curves, I felt very strongly that if someone's been waiting thirty years to see John Fogerty sing "Born on the Bayou," then it better sound like what he thinks "Born on the Bayou" should sound like and not an acoustic guitar and tambourine.

[The *Blue Moon Swamp* tour] was exhilarating. When I look around, I don't see that many guys at my stage of the game touring that much. The class seems to be crowded with twenty-year-olds. So I have to ask myself, "Why am I doing this?" And the answer is, "Because I love it." I waited a long time and feel I have a lot left to prove. Which isn't to say that I have something deep and profound to tell everybody, just that since I've been away so much the desire to get the music out and perform in front of people has been frustrated, like I was in suspended animation. It's kind of like when Muhammad Ali got banned from the ring for all those years, but when he came back, he was in really great shape. I always thought that I was a good musician and I'm also really competitive, but if you're not making new records and you're not on TV, how the heck are people going to know you're out there? So I feel like I'm kind of a new kid now.

The shows were amazing. When we came out and would start with "Born on the Bayou," right in the first few seconds of the song, this feeling would come up from the audience. I don't know whether it was love or joy or just that these people were really damn happy that this was happening. I didn't count on that. I just thought I would do the best job I could and maybe get a pat on the back. Like every other entertainer, I just wanted some approval. But this thing happened and it kept happening during the whole tour. I remember once during "Proud Mary" seeing this guy standing in the audience, smiling, singing the words with tears coming down his face. And during the meet-and-greets after the show people would say, "I just never thought I would see John Fogerty sing 'Proud Mary' in my lifetime." There was a lot of emotion there.

I had thought about recording a live album for years in a general way. [CCR's] live-recording history was kind of checkered. We recorded that show with Tom Donahue that was meant to be a TV special. It was not meant to be a movie, it was not meant to be an album. But it turned out to be a very good live recording of Creedence Clearwater. I was in charge of that whole production at the time. A couple of years later, Fantasy released the *Live in Europe* album, which really stunk up the joint as far as I'm concerned. So that was the first thing that was released, that came out as a live album over my protest. Doug and Stu had allowed the record company to pay for the recording as opposed to having us pay for it. That meant Fantasy owned the tapes, but we ended up having to pay for it anyway since they deducted it from our royalties. And then we didn't have claim to ownership so we couldn't say no. It reflected the trio in all its banal glory.

Many years later, Fantasy released the live recording that had been done as the TV special. At first they called it *Live at Albert Hall*, but they finally 'fessed up that it had been recorded at the Oakland Coliseum. The vinyl record was actually pretty good, but I've since listened to the CD that was released and somebody did something to the tape, because the sound is really, really bad. It sounds like it's in a big canyon. All you can get out of it is that that John Fogerty sings hard. I just can't understand what he's saying. It's like a bad nightmare.

The suggestion [to make *Premonition*] was made by [Warner Brothers chairman] Russ Thyret, the CEO of the label, and the timing was great. It was right at the start of the tour last year. I was at the House of Blues here in LA for the first of three shows. He came to the first two shows, but on the night between, he went to the Fleetwood Mac taping and he came back to me and he said, "Man, I know what we should do." He came to the show not really expecting what he might see. Let's face it,

John Fogerty had been out of the limelight for years and years and years and his records, though of mythical properties, had been off the charts forever. He got what I am immediately. He saw an exciting performance and he saw a guy really having a great time at the top of his game. His imagination was fueled and he told me about his idea and I agreed with him. Because what the tour reflected was a guy coming home, a guy who's finally gotten his whole life's work together, that he's comfortable, maybe even prideful, of who and what he is.

I always hoped that doing a live recording would give me the chance to revisit my older stuff in a new way, the stuff I did in the Creedence days. I have this sort of strange duality to my existence, which is to say I am the "Artist Formerly Known as Creedence Clearwater Revival." I've come to terms with that, but other people sometimes put John Fogerty in competition with that guy in Creedence, which is silly. It's the same guy. He's singing the songs that he wrote, and I've long thought that the best way to reclaim those songs would be with a live album. The old John and the new John are really the same guy. (1998)

DISCOGRAPHY

Singles

Tommy Fogerty and the Blue Velvets
"Come On Baby"/ "Oh My Love" (Orchestra) 1961
"Have You Ever Been Lonely"/ "Bonita" (Orchestra) 1961
"Now You're Not Mine"/ "Yes You Did" (Orchestra) 1962

The Golliwogs
"Don't Tell Me No Lies"/ "Little Girl, Does Your Mama Know?"
   (Fantasy) 1964
"Where You Been"/ "You Came Walking" (Fantasy) 1965
"You Got Nothin' on Me"/ "You Can't Be True" (Fantasy) 1965
"Brown-Eyed Girl"/ "You Better Be Careful" (Scorpio) 1966
"Fight Fire"/ "Fragile Child" (Scorpio) 1966
"Walking on the Water"/ "You Better Get It Before It Gets You"
   (Scorpio) 1966

Creedence Clearwater Revival

"Porterville"/ "Call It Pretending" (Scorpio) 1968

"Suzie Q (Part One)"/ "Suzie Q" (Part Two)" (Fantasy) 1968

"I Put a Spell on You"/ "Walking on the Water" (Fantasy) 1968

"Proud Mary"/ "Born on the Bayou" (Fantasy) 1969

"Bad Moon Rising"/ "Lodi" (Fantasy) 1969

"Green River"/ "Commotion" (Fantasy) 1969

"Down on the Corner"/ "Fortunate Son" (Fantasy) 1969

"Travelin' Band"/ "Who'll Stop the Rain" (Fantasy) 1970

"Up Around the Bend"/ "Run Through the Jungle" (Fantasy) 1970

"Lookin' Out My Back Door"/ "Long As I Can See the Light" (Fantasy) 1970

"Have You Ever Seen the Rain?"/ "Hey Tonight" (Fantasy) 1971

"Sweet Hitch-Hiker"/ "Door to Door" (Fantasy) 1971

"Someday Never Comes"/ "Tearin' Up the Country" (Fantasy) 1972

"I Heard It Through the Grapevine"/ "Good Golly Miss Molly" (Fantasy) 1976

"Tombstone Shadow"/ "Commotion" (Fantasy) 1981

"Cotton Fields"/ "Lodi" (Fantasy) 1981

Note: Fantasy also released several promotional singles, including medleys of CCR hits.

Blue Ridge Rangers

"Blue Ridge Mountain Blues"/ "Have Thine Own Way, Lord" (Fantasy) 1972

"Jambalaya (On the Bayou)"/ "Workin' on a Building" (Fantasy) 1972

"Hearts of Stone"/ "Somewhere Listening" (Fantasy) 1973

"Back in the Hills"/ "You Don't Own Me" (Fantasy) 1973

John Fogerty
"Rockin' All Over the World"/ "The Wall" (Asylum) 1975
"Almost Saturday Night"/ "Sea Cruise" (Asylum) 1975
"You Got the Magic"/ "Evil Thing" (Asylum) 1976
"The Old Man Down the Road"/ "Big Train from Memphis" (Warner Brothers) 1985
"Rock and Roll Girls"/ "Centerfield" (Warner Brothers) 1985
"Eye of the Zombie"/ "I Confess" (Warner Brothers) 1986
"Change in the Weather"/ "My Toot Toot" (Warner Brothers) 1986
"Walkin' in a Hurricane" (Warner Brothers) 1997
"Blue Boy" (Warner Brothers) 1997
"Premonition" (Warner Brothers) 1998

Tom Fogerty
"Goodbye Media Man (Part One)"/ "Goodbye Media Man (Part Two)" (Fantasy) 1971
"Cast the First Stone"/ "Lady of Fatima" (Fantasy) 1972
"Faces, Places, People"/ "Forty Years" (Fantasy) 1972
"Joyful Resurrection"/ "Heartbeat" (Fantasy) 1973
"Mystic Isle Avalon"/ "Reggie" (Fantasy) 1973
"Money,"/ "It's Been a Good Day" (Fantasy) 1974
"Sweet Things to Come" (Fantasy) 1975
"Judy Lee"/ "Baby, What You Want Me To Do?" (Fantasy) 1975
"Life Is But a Dream"/ "Running Back to Me" (Fantasy) 1976
"Champagne Love"/ "The Secret" (Fantasy) 1981

Doug Clifford
"Latin Music"/ "Take a Train" (Fantasy) 1972

Don Harrison Band (with Doug Clifford and Stu Cook)
"Rock 'n' Roll Records"/ "Dancing Girl" (Atlantic) 1976
"Sixteen Tons"/ "Who I Really Am" (Atlantic) 1976

Sir Douglas Quintet (with Doug Clifford and Stu Cook)
"Meet Me in Stockholm"/ "Charisma Face" (Sonet) 1983

Albums

The Golliwogs
Pre-Creedence (Fantasy) 1975

Creedence Clearwater Revival
Creedence Clearwater Revival (Fantasy) 1968
Bayou Country (Fantasy) 1969
Green River (Fantasy) 1969
Willy and the Poor Boys (Fantasy) 1969
Cosmo's Factory (Fantasy) 1970
Pendulum (Fantasy) 1970
Mardi Gras (Fantasy) 1972
Creedence Gold (Fantasy) 1972
More Creedence Gold (Fantasy) 1973
Live in Europe (Fantasy) 1973
Chronicle (Fantasy) 1976
The Royal Albert Hall Concert (Fantasy) 1980; retitled *The Concert* when
   Fantasy acknowledged that the tapes of the "Royal Albert Hall" con-
   cert had been recorded in Oakland
Chronicle, Volume 2 (Fantasy) 1987

Blue Ridge Rangers
The Blue Ridge Rangers (Fantasy) 1973

John Fogerty
John Fogerty (Asylum) 1975
Hoodoo (Asylum) 1976; never released, withdrawn several days before
  scheduled release
Centerfield (Warner Brothers) 1985
Eye of the Zombie (Warner Brothers) 1986
Blue Moon Swamp (Warner Brothers) 1997
Premonition (Reprise) 1998

Doug Clifford
Doug "Cosmo" Clifford (Fantasy) 1972

Tom Fogerty
Tom Fogerty (Fantasy) 1972
Excalibur (Fantasy) 1972
Zephyr National (Fantasy) 1974
Myopia (Fantasy) 1974
Ruby (PBR) 1976
Rock and Roll Madness (PBR) 1978
Deal It Out (Fantasy) 1981
Precious Gems (Fantasy) 1984
Sidekicks (Fantasy) 1992

Merl Saunders (with Tom Fogerty)
Heavy Turbulence 1972

Fire Up 1973
Live at Keystone

Don Harrison Band (with Stu Cook and Doug Clifford)
Don Harrison Band (Atlantic) 1976
Red Hot (Atlantic) 1976
Not Far From Free (Mercury) 1977

Southern Pacific
Killbilly Hill (Warner)
Zuma (Warner)
County Line (Warner)
Greatest Hits (Warner)

Sir Douglas Quintet
Groover's Paradise (Warner) 1974
Midnight Sun (Sonet) 1983
Day Dreaming at Midnight (Elektra) 1994

Creedence Clearwater Revisited
Recollection (Poor Boy) 1998

SOURCES

Anon. "John Fogerty: Lead Guitarist/Creedence Clearwater Revival," *Hitparader* (July 1969), p. 23.

Carpenter, John. "Creedence Clearwater Revival," *Hitparader Yearbook* (1971), p. 35.

Carr, Roy. "Creedence Clearwater Revival Are Really an Eleven Piece Group," *Hitparader* (January 1971), pp. 35-36.

"Creedence Clearwater Revival: Long Live Rock and Roll," *Hitparader* (September 1969), pp. 54-57.

"Creedence Clearwater Revival: Tom, Stu and Doug," *Hitparader* (January 1970), pp. 20-21.

"The Creedence Rhythm Section," *Hitparader* (January 1970), p. 23.

"Creedence Splits: No More Chooglin'," *Rolling Stone* (November 9, 1972), p. 6.

DiMartino, Dave. "Swamp Thing," *Rolling Stone* (June 26, 1997), p. 23.

Dubro, Alec. Review of *Willy and the Poor Boys*. *Rolling Stone* (January 21, 1970), p. 44.

Fantasy Inc, Plaintiff, v. John C. Fogerty, Wenaha Music Co.,Warner

Bros. Records Inc., WEA International, Inc., Defendants. Transcript of testimony presented in the United States District Court for the Northern District of California. Case number C 85-4929-SC.

Fantasy Records v. John Fogerty. Transcript of deposition submitted to U.S. District Court, San Francisco, California. Ref. number PO588-2.

Fogerty, John. "My Favorite Records," *Hitparader* (September 1969), p. 58.

Fogerty, Tom. "Creedence Clearwater Revival: Tom Fogerty Relates Its Evolution," *Goldmine* (May 24, 1985), pp. 22-24.

Fong-Torres, Ben. "Creedence Clearwater At the Hop," *Rolling Stone* (April 5, 1969), p. 9.

Friedland, Ed. "Stu Cook: Back to the Trenches," *Bass Player* (April 1998), pp. 20-22.

Gleason, Ralph J. "The Rolling Stone Interview: John Fogerty," *Rolling Stone* (February 21, 1970), pp. 17-24.

Goldberg, Michael. "Fortunate Son," *Rolling Stone* (February 4, 1993), pp. 47-48, 77.

"John Fogerty of Creedence—'Rock Is Still the Foundation'," *Hitparader* (February 1972), pp. 25-26, 44.

"John Fogerty on the New Album," *Hitparader* (January 1970), pp. 55-57.

Lernoux, Penny. *In Banks We Trust* (New York: Viking, 1986).

Levitin, Daniel. "The Audio Interview: John Fogerty," *Audio* (January 1998), pp. 38-45.

Lombardi, John. "Creedence Clearwater Throws Serious Party," *Rolling Stone* (January 7, 1971), pp. 5-6.

Marsh, Dave. *The Heart of Rock and Soul* (New York: Plume, 1989).

Reeds, Dafydd, and Luke Crampton. *The Encyclopedia of Rock Stars* (New York: DK Publishing, 1996).

Robinson, Richard. "West Coast Rocker: John Fogerty," *Hitparader* (March 1970), pp. 56-57.

Selvin, Joel. "Creedence Got a Kinda New Bag," *Rolling Stone* (December 24, 1970), p. 6.

Settle, Ken. "Creedence Clearwater Revival, *The Bayou and Backstreets*," *Goldmine* (June 8, 1984), pp. 6-18.

Song Hits magazine "Creedence Clearwater Revival" special issue (Summer 1971).

"The Strength of Creedence Is Creedence," *Hitparader* (April 1972), p. 24.

"Tom Fogerty," *Hitparader* (January 1972), p. 28.

"Tom Fogerty Dies," *Rolling Stone* (November 11, 1990), p. 16.

"Tom Fogerty Leaves Creedence," *Rolling Stone* (March 4, 1971), p. 16.

"The Triumphant Return of John Fogerty," *Addicted to Noise* issue 3.05, cover story.

Werner, Craig. "The Return of John Fogerty," *Goldmine* (July 18, 1997), pp. 16-19, 38-48, 54-62.

"Will Creedence Clearwater Ever Be Revived?," *Rolling Stone* (September 2, 1982), p. 41.

INDEX

A

Albert Hall, 113
"Almost Saturday Night," 179
Amalgamated American
International FM Workers
of the World, 69
"Annie Had a Baby," 37, 158,
191
Apostles, 45
Arnold, Edward, 175
Aronoff, Kenny, 226
Asylum Records, 175, 178,
179–180
Atkins, Chet, 17
Atlantic/Stax, 87
Avalon Ballroom, 84

B

Bad Meat, 189
"Bad Moon Rising," 2, 25, 72,
82, 88, 97, 99, 117, 134,
140, 141, 144
Baker, LaVern, 81
Ballard, Hank, 158
Bayou Country, 82, 86, 94, 172
Beatles, 86–87, 134
"Be-Bop-A-Lulu," 144

"Before You Accuse Me," 36
Belafonte, Harry, 16
"Believe What You Say," 25
Bennett, Tony, 27
Berkeley Barb, 120
Berry, Chuck, 5, 13, 16, 19,
22, 24, 100, 196
"Beverly Angel," 34
Bishop, Elvin, 157
"Blue Boy, 224
"Blue Moon Nights," 153
"Blue Moon Rising," 224
Blue Moon Swamp, 153, 224,
225, 226, 227, 228, 229
Blue Ridge Rangers, 174, 176,
177, 178
"Blues in C," 162
"Blues in G," 16, 162
"Blue Suede Shoes," 25
Blue Velvets, 24, 31, 34, 35,
38, 39, 42, 191
Blue Violets, 31
"Bonita," 36
Booker T. and the MGs, 8, 87,
111, 112, 210
"Born on the Bayou," 72, 84,
85, 98, 218, 227, 228, 229

Bowie, David, 225
Boyer, LaNada, 121, 122
Brooks, Garth, 153
Brown, James, 13, 37, 70, 145,
149
"Brown-Eyed Girl," 32, 46,
47, 48, 49, 76
"Bulldog," 36
Bumble Boogie," 16
Burke, Solomon, 143
Burnstein, Malcolm, 197
Burton, James, 8, 17–18, 22,
25, 70, 177
Butterfield, Paul, Blues Band,
59, 78, 80
Byrnes, Mike, 39

C

Cannon, Viola, 210
Carlos, 61
Carousel, 64
Cash, Johnny, 215
Castillo, Edward, 121, 122
"Cast Your Fate to the Wind,"
40–41
Centerfield, 175, 194, 195, 207,
226

"Centerfield," 72, 150, 194
Charles, Ray, 8, 13, 19, 36, 70
Charles, Sonny, 143
Checker, Chubby, 39
Checkmates, 143
Chiffons, 196
The Chords, 36
Christian, Charlie, 36
Christy Records, 34
Clifford, Doug, 1, 5, 10, 18,
    19, 23–24, 32, 34, 38, 43,
    44, 46, 47, 49, 50–51, 52,
    53, 61–62, 74, 84, 85, 88,
    89, 101, 103, 114–116,
    125–126, 127–128, 129,
    131, 139, 155, 158,
    160–161, 162, 163, 165,
    166, 169–171, 173, 176,
    187–188, 191, 192, 193,
    204–206, 217, 218–221,
    222–225, 230
Close Encounters of the Third
    Kind, 225
"Come on Baby," 35
"Commotion," 146
Como, Perry, 19
Cook, Stu, 1, 2, 3, 4, 5, 18–19,
    22–23, 24, 32, 43, 46, 47,
    53, 59, 62–64, 67–68, 71,
    73, 74, 76, 80, 82, 84,
    85–86, 88–89, 90, 93–94,
    97–98, 101, 102–103, 107,
    108, 112–114, 119,
    122–123, 124–125,
    128–130, 131, 136–137,
    139, 155, 158, 159,
    162–163, 164–168, 171,
    176, 188–191, 192, 206,
    217–218, 219, 220, 222,
    223, 230
Cooke, Sam, 215
Corvette, Johnny, and the
    Corvettes, 14–15, 99, 116
Cosmo's Factory, 99, 100, 127,

137, 186, 188
Cosmo's Factory, 128, 129–130,
    150
"Cotton Fields," 100
Crewcuts, 81
Cropper, Steve, 70, 83
Crosby, Leon, 68
Crows and Five Royals, 22,
    25, 36

D

Davis, Gary, 70
Dees, Rick, 66
Del-Fi Records, 35, 171
Deno and Carlo's, 59, 69, 77,
    80, 81, 85
Diamonds, 81
Diddley, Bo, 16, 22, 24, 36,
    84, 142
DiSousa, Bob, 38
Dixon, Willie, 140
Domino, Fats, 23–24, 84, 134
Donahue, Rachel, 64, 65,
    68–69, 69–70, 111–112
Donahue, Tom, 64, 68, 69,
    111, 230
"Don't Look Now," 148
Dorsey, Thomas, 140
Douglas, Jerry, 177, 216, 217
"Down on the Corner," 2, 97,
    99, 100, 116, 117, 118
"Do You Wanna Dance?", 165
Drake, Bill, 76, 79
"Dream Baby," 145
Drifters, 39
"Drown in My Own Tears,"
    36
Dryden, Spencer, 62
Dunn, Duck, 97, 188, 210
Dylan, Bob, 109, 140

E

Eagle, Adam Fortunate, 123
"Earth Angel," 36

"East-West," 78
Eddy, Duane, 16, 17, 18, 22,
    25, 33, 70
Elliot, Jack, 17
Ellison, Ralph, 3, 225
"Endless Sleep," 15
Engel, Barrie, 175
Evans, Susan, 219
Everly Brothers, 72
Eye of the Zombie, 127, 175,
    177, 195, 196, 225

F

Fanning, Tom, 39
Fantasy Records, 31, 39,
    40–41, 46, 52, 55, 130, 134,
    169–170, 174, 176,
    177–178, 179, 181, 187,
    193, 230
Farlow, Wayne, 35
Feather, Leonard, 214
"Fight Fire," 46, 76
Fillmore West, 1, 59, 64, 67,
    106
Fina, Jack, 16
"Fireballs," 25
Fire Up, 181
Fleetwood Mac, 80
Fogerty, Jeff, 219
Fogerty, John, 1–2, 3, 5, 6,
    8–9, 13–18, 21–23, 24–27,
    32, 33–34, 36–38, 39–40,
    39–41, 42–55, 56, 57,
    60–61, 66, 67, 68, 69,
    70–73, 76–81, 82–85,
    86–88, 89, 91–93, 94–97,
    101–102, 106, 107,
    108–111, 112, 113,
    116–119, 120–122,
    123–124, 126–127,
    130–131, 135, 138,
    140–164, 169, 171,
    172–173, 174–181, 186,
    191, 192, 193, 195–204,

205, 207–208, 208–217, 222, 225–231
Fogerty, Julie, 152–153
Fogerty, Tom, 1, 5, 7, 14, 22, 27–29, 31, 34–36, 38–39, 42, 46–47, 48, 49, 53, 54, 56, 58, 66–67, 68, 70–71, 88, 90, 135, 156–158, 159, 165–166, 171, 182, 183–184, 186, 191, 192
"Fortunate Son," 3, 11, 100, 116, 123, 125, 144, 224, 227
Francoise, Ray, 88, 128
Freeman, Bobby, 165
Freeman, Ernie, 16
Free Speech Movement, 45, 67–68

G

Gable, Clark, 28
Garcia, Jerry, 5, 65, 70, 157, 181, 184
Gary, Russ, 86, 188–189
"Gee," 36
Geffen, David, 175, 178–179
"Get Down Woman," 79
Gibbs, Georgia, 81
Gleason, Ralph, 58, 59, 60, 81, 141
"God Save the Queen," 113
Golliwogs, 31, 32, 39, 41, 42, 43, 44, 46, 53, 55, 56, 62, 64, 68, 164
"Good Golly Miss Molly," 86, 197
Goodman, Benny, 8
Gordy, Berry, 2
Graham, Bill, 62, 64, 69
Grateful Dead, 5, 58, 59, 60, 61, 62, 65, 69, 101, 102, 157
"Graveyard Train," 85
"Green Onions," 32, 37, 38
Green River, 86, 93–94, 99, 116, 130

"Green River," 2, 9, 11, 72, 82, 100, 116, 117, 145–146, 151, 224
Guaraldi, Vince, 41

H

Haggard, Merle, 58, 153
Harrison, Don, 186, 188–189
Harrison, Don, Band, 5
Havens, Richie, 87
"Have You Ever Been Lonely?", 36
"Have You Seen the Rain?", 2, 156
Hawkins, Dale, 25, 59, 76
Hawkins, Tremaine, 185
Hawkins, Walter, 8, 185, 188
Heavy Turbulence, 181, 185
Hendrix, Jimi, 25, 137, 149
Hentoff, Nat, 214
"He's So Fine," 196
"Hill and Gully Rider," 16
Hinton, Sam, 14, 17
Holly, Buddy, 13, 35, 98, 100, 144, 215
"Honky Tonk," 37
Hoodoo, 175, 179
Hooker, John Lee, 210
Hopkins, Lightnin', 17
"Hot Rod Heart," 224
Howlin' Wolf, 19, 22, 28, 39, 40, 66, 80, 81, 82, 209
"Hully Gully," 32, 37, 191
"A Hundred and Ten in the Shade," 151–152
"Hush Your Mouth," 36

I

"I Heard It Through the Grapevine," 129, 149
"I'm a Man," 36
"In Concert," 112
"In the Midnight Hour," 77, 112

"I Put a Spell on You," 60, 78, 79
"I Saw It on TV," 150
"It Came Out of the Sky," 140, 148
"It's a Long Way to Tiperarry," 15

J

Jackson, Al, 111, 112
Jackson, Mahalia, 9
Jagger, Mick, 109
Jefferson Airplane, 58, 59, 60, 62, 63, 65, 70, 137
Johnny and the Hurricanes, 33
Johnson, Robert, 8, 9, 209, 210
"Joy of My Life," 152–153

K

Kaffel, Ralph, 54
Kanter, Burton, 175
Kasem, Casey, 35–36
Kaukonen, Jorma, 70
"Keep on Chooglin'," 85, 113
Keltner, Jim, 220
King, B. B., 28, 37, 70, 87, 107
Kingston Trio, 16
Kirschner, Don, 112
Knudsen, Keith, 189
Kourtz, Bruce, 88, 128
Kweskin, Jim, 146

L

"La Bamba," 165, 171
Landau, Jon, 156, 163
The Last Days of the Fillmore, 65
"Last Time," 76
Leadbelly, 1, 99–100
Lewis, Jerry Lee, 13, 24–25, 84
Lightnin' Hopkins, 14

Lion's Share, 59
Lipscomb, Mance, 14, 17
Little Richard, 13, 23, 24, 40,
    100, 197
Little Walter, 30
Live at Albert Hall, 230
Live at Keystone, 185
Live in Europe, 230
"Lodi," 32, 43, 88, 141, 143,
    144
Lomax, Alan, 118
"Long As I Can See the
    Light," 156
"Long Cool Woman," 144
"Lookin' Out My Back
    Door," 82, 99, 130, 153,
    156
"Lost Dreams," 16
"Louie Louie," 1, 32, 37
"Lyda Jane," 35

M

Madonna, 225
Mardi Gras, 155, 156, 163,
    167, 168
Marsh, Dave, 5, 31–32, 224
Martin, Freddy, 16
Mason, John, 189–190
McCracklin, Jimmy, 19
McPhatter, Clyde, 39
McPhee, John, 188, 189
"Media Man," 182, 183
Memphis Sun Records, 24
Midnighters, 70
"Midnight Hour," 37
"Midnight Special, 99–100
Miller, Steve, Band, 137
Mitchell, Joni, 141
"Moanin' in the Moonlight,"
    28
Moby Grape, 58, 60, 63, 137
Monkees, 47
Monkey Inn, 45–46
Moore, Scotty, 22, 25

Morrison, Van, 87
Motown, 134
"Mr Greed," 204
Murray, Albert, 225
"Mustang Sally," 37
"My Babe," 158
"My Sweet Lord," 196

N

Nelson, Ricky, 8, 18, 25, 134
New Monrk, 59
"The Night They Drove Old
    Dixie Down," 158

O

Oakes, Richard, 122
"Oh My Love," 35
"The Old Man Down the
    Road," 150, 168, 175, 194,
    195, 196–197, 199, 202,
    203
"One Hundred and Ten in the
    Shade," 216, 224
"Ooby Dooby," 129
Orbison, Roy, 145
Orchestra Records, 35
Osmond Brothers, 61
Owens, Buck, 58, 153

P

Page, Patti, 27
Patton, Charlie, 8, 210–211,
    212
Pendulum, 155, 156
Pendulum, 86, 156
Penguins, 36
"Penthouse Pauper," 142
Perkins, Carl, 16, 22, 24, 25,
    30, 84, 153, 174
Phillips, John, 66
Pickett, Wilson, 40, 87
Pig, Tony, 60
"Pipeline," 36–37
Playboys, 31, 34–35

Porter, Cole, 28
"Porterville," 51
Powell, James, 34
Premonition, 224, 230
"Premonition," 153–154
Presley, Elvis, 1, 9, 13, 17, 22,
    100, 106, 134, 143, 153,
    213
"Proud Mary," 1, 59, 82, 83,
    85, 86, 88, 99, 110, 116,
    124, 140, 141–142, 143,
    144, 191, 210, 218, 227,
    229, 230

Q

Quicksilver Messenger
    Service, 58, 60
Quintet, Sir Douglas, 5, 186

R

"Rambunctious Boy," 153
"Rawhide," 36
Red Cold and Ready to Fold, 188
Redding, Otis, 19, 87
Red Hot, 188
"Red River Valley," 15
Reed, Jimmy, 22, 210
Revere, Paul, 32, 39
Reynolds, Jody, 15
"Riverboat," 141
Robertson, Robbie, 218, 220
"Rock and Roll Girls," 194
Rock and Roll Hall of Fame,
    214–215, 217
"Rockin' All Over the
    World," 179
Rohrer, Jake, 88, 89, 128, 168
Rohrer, Mary, 128
"Rolling on the River," 141
Rolling Stone, 116, 141
Ross, Diana, 134
"Run Through the Jungle," 2,
    98, 100, 123, 126, 144, 175,
    195, 198, 205, 206

S

Sam and Dave, 87
"San Antonio Rose," 15
Santana, 61, 137
"Satisfaction," 76
Saunders, Merl, 5, 8, 41–42, 64, 65, 76, 181, 182, 184–186
Saunders-Garcia Band, 185
Scorpio Records, 46
"Searchlight," 150
Sebastian, John, 188
Seeger, Pete, 14, 17
"See That My Grave Is Kept Clean," 158
Selah, 185
Sevareid, Eric, 120
Sgt. Pepper, 87
"Sh-Boom," 36
"Shep" album, 175, 179
Sidle, Ken, 197
Sierra Sound, 38
"Sing, Sing, Sing," 146
"Sinister Purpose," 147
"Sixteen Tons," 188
"Slippin' and Slidin'," 158
"Slummer the Slum," 25–26
Sly and the Family Stone, 137
Smith, Joe, 74, 180
"Smokestack Lightnin'," 28
"Someday Never Comes," 2, 149–150, 156
Southern Pacific, 5, 186, 189
"Southern Streamline," 151, 224
Spector, Phil, 66
"Spell," 77, 78
"Spoonful," 28
Springsteen, Bruce, 2, 9, 140, 217, 220
Staples, Pop, 36
Stax Studios, 2
Stealum, Morris, 209
Stone, Sly, 2

Sun Records, 17, 84, 162–163
"Surfin' U.S.A.", 196
"Susie Q," 25, 32, 59, 60, 74, 76, 77, 78, 79, 81, 84, 94–95, 98, 172
Swallowtail, T. Spicebush, 46
"Swamp River Days," 9, 151, 224
"Sweet Little Sixteen," 196

T

Taj Mahal, 63
"Tell the Truth," 36
"Three Thirty Blues," 16, 70
"Tombstone Shadow," 147
"Tom Dooley," 16
"Torquay," 25
"Travelin' Band," 82, 197
Travis, Merle, 188
Tristao, John, 190
"Tubby the Tuba," 15
Tumato, Duke, 226
Turner, Ike, 143
Turner, Tina, 143, 144
"Turn on Your Love Light," 101

U

"Up Around the Bend," 2, 72, 99, 100

V

Valens, Richie, 3, 165, 171
"Vanz Kant Danz," 175, 198, 200
Ventures, 18, 25, 33
Vince Guaraldi Trio, 40–41
Vincent, Gene, 144
"Violence Is Golden," 127
Viscounts, 34
Visions, 31, 41, 42, 53

W

Wailers, 34
"Walk Don't Run," 32

"Walking in a Hurricane," 224
"Walking on the Water," 46, 47
Warner Brothers, 194
Waronker, Lenny, 194, 204
Waters, Muddy, 9, 19, 27, 30, 88, 209, 210, 213–214
Webb, Spyder, and the Insects, 31, 34, 35
Weiss, Max, 41, 42, 46, 54
Weiss, Sol, 41, 42
Wheat, Peter, and the Breadmen, 61
"Who'll Stop the Rain," 2, 3, 5, 98, 100, 125, 130, 140, 148–149, 218
Willy and the Poor Boys, 99, 100, 116, 117, 224
Wilson, Jackie, 70
Winter, Edgar, 157
Winter, Johnny, 157
Winterland, 64, 67
Winwood, Steve, 69, 87
"Wipe Out," 37, 39
"The Working Man," 79
"WPLJ," 158
"Wrote a Song for Everyone," 9, 11, 140, 147–148

Y

"Yes You Did," 36
Young, Bruce, 128

Z

Zaentz, Saul, 32, 42, 52, 54, 55–56, 77, 78, 130, 135–136, 169, 176, 184, 192, 200–201, 205, 206, 207, 209, 218, 228
"Zanz Kant Danz," 175, 198, 200, 201, 204
Zeppelin, Led, 134

CRAIG WERNER teaches in the Department of Afro-American Studies at the University of Wisconsin. His books include *A Change Is Gonna Come: Music, Race and the Soul of America* and *Playing the Changes: From Afro-Modernism to the Jazz Impulse*. A native of Colorado, he acquired first-hand knowledge of the CCR repertoire while playing in the garage band Armageddon. He lives in Madison, Wisconsin, with his wife, Leslee Nelson, and their daughters, Riah and Kaylee Werner.

DAVE MARSH was a founding editor of *Creem* and an editor at *Rolling Stone*, where he created the *The Rolling Stone Record Guide*. He is now a music critic at *Playboy*, publisher of *Rock & Rap Confidential*, and a prolific author of books about music and popular culture, including books about Elvis Presley, Michael Jackson, and the song "Louie Louie." His book *Before I Get Old* is the definitive biography of the Who, and *Glory Days* and *Born to Run*, both about Bruce Springsteen, were best-sellers.